A LIFE
Transformed
SALLY JEFFREE

Published in 2021

Published for Sally Jeffree by Verité CM Limited,
124 Sea Place, Worthing, West Sussex BN12 4BG
+44 (0) 1903 241975

email: enquiries@veritecm.com
Web: www.veritecm.com

British Library Cataloguing in Publication Data
A record for this book is available from The British Library

ISBN: 978-1-914388-07-1

Cover Photo by Wesley Msamange
"I Was a Stranger"
Food for 350 People Living on a Rubbish Dump

Printed in the UK

Contents

Chapter 1

A Life-Transforming Decision

John 10:7-10: "[7] Therefore Jesus said again, 'Very truly I tell you,
I am the gate for the sheep. [8] All who have come before me are
thieves and robbers, but the sheep have not listened to them.
[9] I am the gate; whoever enters through me will be saved.
They will come in and go out, and find pasture. [10] The thief comes
only to steal and kill and destroy; I have come that they may have
life, and have it to the full.'"

Many people have suggested that I should write a testimony of the miraculous experiences that I have seen over the last thirty-four years, but I did not want to do so without the clear leading of the Holy Spirit. One of the many lessons which I have learnt is that any action taken without His clear leading is futile in terms of spiritual significance and that my ability to achieve anything without Him is extremely limited. However, having recently received two clear and encouraging words to do this, I am now trusting that my efforts to recall the events and lessons of these years will produce some positive benefits and blessings to those who may read these words.

Personal testimonies are very powerful. They not only encourage us all to trust more in the awesome and wonderful faithfulness of God, teaching us that God continues to perform similar miracles to those we find in the Bible, but they should also give us the opportunity to learn from the experience of others as they have learned to live according to the principles set out so clearly in His Word. This is one important purpose of writing this book.

Aged nearly seventy-five, I have come to a place where I feel that I have just started to live the abundant and blessed life that Jesus promised us in the above quoted verse from the gospel of John. This had not been true up until recently. Having been locked up as a punishment when I was very young and having faced emotional abuse from early school years onwards, my past was blighted by considerable anxiety and a lack of self-confidence which led me to allow even more abuse from a variety of different people.

Now everything is completely different. I have a very deep confidence in God's love for me which has changed everything. All the anxiety has gone. To use a modern term: I feel comfortable in my own skin. My relationships with other people have changed dramatically and I feel a deep and sustained inner joy every day, regardless of a whole variety of difficulties and frustrations which I still face. To sum it up: life is wonderful.

I now feel a burden to share the lessons which I have learned with others so that they can experience the same sustained abundance and joy that I enjoy. Sometimes, healing can be instant but most of us face a complex mixture of different wounds which will take time to change. For me, it has taken forty-one years, but for others this process could be much shorter, especially with the benefit of applying the lessons which others have learned.

This liberating and healing process began during November 1977 when I made the most crucial decision of my life, a decision that would transform my life beyond anything that I could have ever imagined at the time. I was thirty-four years old. Earlier that year, I had met a lady who had three young children and whose husband was serving in the army in Germany. Her husband was due to leave the army in a few months' time and my newly found friend had come back to the UK to secure a council house for the whole family to live in when his time of service finished.

On one of my regular visits to her home, I found her in the utmost despair. She had just received a letter from her husband admitting to adultery and asking for a divorce. This was not only a very severe emotional blow, but it also caused her considerable financial insecurity and concern with three children to look after. I would have liked to encourage her but did not know what to say. The situation looked very bleak. However, when I returned to visit her about a week later, she was radiantly happy. I asked whether her circumstances had changed. She said that they had not but that she had become a Christian.

I knew immediately that she had discovered something that I wanted desperately and for which I had been searching without success for most of my life. We all want to be happy and fulfilled but for most of us this seemingly simple goal remains frustratingly elusive. I was very curious and asked her lots of questions because my childhood church attendance had never made me happy. In fact, as soon as I was old enough to make my own decisions, I had stopped going. She was not able to answer most of my questions but lent me a book written by the singer Pat Boone, in which he had written the testimony of his own conversion experience.

It would not be an exaggeration to say that I devoured this book hungrily. It was a little like a treasure hunt where I had caught a glimpse of a priceless gift and I now needed to discover how to find it. I cannot remember – some forty years later – much of the contents of this book but I do remember that it taught me that Christianity is not simply about attending church but about a personal relationship with God which has been made possible for us through Jesus' sacrificial death on the cross. My early church and Sunday school attendance had taught me the basic facts about and reasons for Jesus' crucifixion. However, I had no idea that it was possible for us to have a personal relationship with God in which He not only desires to transform our lives, healing us from past hurts and filling us with peace and the power of His Holy Spirit, but that we can also learn how to hear His voice guiding us and leading us into the wonderful and abundant life that He has prepared for every one of us.

The truth is that many of us have been wounded and abused by other people who have failed to treat us with the love and acceptance that we desperately need, but God loves us unconditionally and longs to pour His redeeming and life-transforming love into our hearts and lives. Furthermore, God has a personal plan for each one of us, a plan which will develop the gifting that He has given us, and which will satisfy and fulfil our hearts and lives in a way that nothing else can. Jesus confirms this wonderful truth in the passage from the gospel of John which is quoted at the beginning of this chapter.

While I was reading Pat Boone's book, my friend was reading a book about the well-known nineteenth-century American Presbyterian minister and leader in the Second Great Awakening in the United States, Charles Finney, and she shared one very significant passage from this book with me. Apparently, each time that he held a public evangelistic crusade and asked those who wanted to receive salvation to come forward at the end of the meeting, he would speak to each one of them and ask them: "Is there anything which you would not do for God?" If, in response, they told him of something which they would not be prepared to do, he would refuse to pray for their salvation, saying that they were not ready to receive Jesus as their Lord and Saviour.

If we read the accounts of where the gospel was presented in the New Testament, the message given by the early believers focused on the life, death, resurrection and lordship of Jesus. This is the good news of the gospel message: "Jesus Christ is Lord". However, if there is anything that we would not be prepared to do for Him, then He is not Lord, and we are still sitting on the throne of our lives. Let us consider why this foundational principle is absolutely essential for a victorious and fruitful life and why the fact that Jesus is Lord is such good news: if we have failed to establish Jesus' lordship in our own lives, how can we trust and believe Him to be Lord over all the opposing and destructive circumstances which we face or the addictions and habits which control us? It is faith in the wonderful truth that Jesus is Lord which sets us free and gives us victory in every situation. We will consider this further in the next chapter.

I learnt more recently that it was the vital importance of this foundational Christian truth that led so many early Christians to face a horrendous death in the Coliseum in Rome at the end of the first century. During this time, Rome ruled much of the land around the Mediterranean and everyone living under their rule was required to confess "Caesar is Lord". This was, of course, abhorrent to Christians who refused in large numbers to do this. As a result, many of them were crucified or fed to lions in the arena with vast crowds watching this barbaric and bloodthirsty spectacle. We can learn from their willingness to die rather than to deny Jesus' lordship, how important they viewed this issue.

Having listened to this passage about Charles Finney, I knew that I needed to come to the point where I would be willing to do whatever God asked of me. To this end, I carefully considered what would be the very worst thing that anyone could possibly ask me to do. At that time, Christians were still being imprisoned in communist Russia because of their refusal to renounce their faith and friends had shared several passages with me from books giving dreadful details of their suffering. Added to the reality and horror of their suffering, I personally suffered from claustrophobia because of being locked up as a punishment when I was a child. The thought of being asked to go to Russia, therefore, filled me with sheer terror. However, I knew that I needed to come to the point where I could honestly say, "Even if you send me to Russia, Lord, I still want You to come into my life as Lord and Saviour."

It took about two weeks of intense inner struggle before I could honestly say this. Shortly after I had done so, the thought, "Read Jeremiah chapter 42", came into my mind. This chapter is about the army officers and all the people of Judah approaching Jeremiah, asking him to pray and to ask the Lord what they should do. The beginning of God's answer is given in verses 9-10a:

> Jeremiah 42:9-10a: "⁹ He said to them, 'This is what the LORD, the
> God of Israel, to whom you sent me to present your petition, says:
> ¹⁰ "If you stay in this land, I will build you up and not tear you
> down; I will plant you and not uproot you."'"

I was relieved, therefore, to know that at least for the foreseeable future, God was not going to send me to Russia! To date, He has never done so. With the benefit of hindsight, I can now see how this one decision was to open the door to such an extraordinary and exciting future. We will consider why this decision to surrender to the lordship of Jesus is essential for our own personal benefit and blessing in the next chapter.

Looking back over the last forty years, I am continually amazed at the exhilarating and fulfilling experiences and opportunities that God has given me and the many miracles which I have seen. In my wildest dreams, I could never have imagined the future that God had in store for me when I made this very difficult decision to surrender my life to Him. I can see now how the blessings which I have received since far outweigh the difficulty and risk of this decision. In fact, as I have prepared to share the amazing story of the last forty years, I find many important lessons which I have learnt, each one of which has opened a new door to further blessings and benefits and all of which far outweigh the difficulty and risk of choosing to follow God's guidance and advice.

The aim of this book is to share my story: the story of how God has transformed a very ordinary and ineffective life and made it extraordinary.

At the same time, I will also share the lessons which I have learnt and the decisions which I have made, without which my life would have continued in its boring and unspectacular way. Many of these choices were irrational and all of them involved some risk but if we hunger for more of God and desire to be fruitful for Him, we need to learn that His ways are not our ways and His thoughts are not our thoughts, and it us who must change!

> Isaiah 55:8-9: "[8] 'For my thoughts are not your thoughts, neither are your ways my ways,' declares the LORD. [9] 'As the heavens are higher than the earth, so are my ways higher than your ways and my thoughts than your thoughts.'"

The lessons which I have learnt over the last forty years show the truth of these verses. God's way is often the exact opposite to the worldly way that we are accustomed to and often appears irrational, risky and filled with danger and uncertainty. It is therefore easy for us to miss God's best because we have a natural tendency to think and to act according to the worldly culture in which we have been raised. It is also true that most of us would prefer to remain in control of our lives and to stay in a place where we feel safe, secure and comfortable. However, I have found that God's way is the only way which will lead to spectacular blessing and benefit, and His way is also far more secure than any plan which we can devise because we live and walk in His presence. If we want to see God's amazing power working in us and through us, we need to learn to think and to act according to biblical truth.

It is possible that you have been a Christian for many years but have not yet seen a tangible demonstration of God's awesome presence and power in your life. I am not suggesting for one moment that your conversion was not genuine, but I do believe that we need to apply God's principles to our lives if we want to walk in His authority, power and fruitfulness. In my experience, it is rather like a staircase with each principle that we apply taking us up to a higher level. I am very aware that I still have much to learn but in this one respect I feel rather like Paul: I know that I have not arrived at my goal, but I continue to press forward towards the prize for which Jesus has taken hold of me.

Philippians 3:12-14: "[12] Not that I have already obtained all this, or have already arrived at my goal, but I press on to take hold of that for which Christ Jesus took hold of me. [13] Brothers and sisters, I do not consider myself yet to have taken hold of it. But one thing I do: forgetting what is behind and straining towards what is ahead, [14] I press on towards the goal to win the prize for which God has called me heavenwards in Christ Jesus."

Chapter 2

Is Jesus Lord?

Romans 10:9: "If you declare with your mouth, 'Jesus is Lord,' and
believe in your heart that God raised him from the dead, you will
be saved."

It has only been with the benefit of hindsight that I have come to understand the very great significance of my first challenge: to surrender to the lordship of Jesus. If we are to better understand the importance of this challenge, we need to consider an important question: what is sin? We will probably answer this question by listing a variety of different sins such as pride, murder, adultery, greed, unforgiveness, etc.; such a list would be extensive. While such an answer is perfectly correct, the main sin, which everyone of us is guilty of, is that of living independently from God, and all the different sins – such as those listed above – are simply the outworking of this one choice of independence. True repentance will therefore require us to give up our independence and the desire to remain in control of our lives and surrender to the lordship of Jesus; depending on Him instead of ourselves. This is the very foundation of the gospel.

Let us consider four reasons why the essential issue of lordship may remain unresolved in many of our Christian lives. First, we so often read the Bible through the distorted lens of our democratic culture. We need to remind ourselves that throughout the period that the Bible was written there was no such thing as a democracy. Nations were ruled by a king (or in the case of Rome, Caesar), and all the people had to submit themselves to his absolute rule over them. The average inhabitant had very few, if any, rights and could be executed at the whim of that king at any time and for no real reason. Let us remember that Jesus taught about the Kingdom of God, not the Democracy of God. I realise that there are still many countries, such as the UK, which still have a king or a queen, but they are symbolic heads of these countries which are ruled by a democratically elected parliament.

When we read the Bible, we need to understand and apply its teaching according to the culture and circumstances within which it was written.

Why is this so very important? It is important because our culture teaches us that we have rights and freedoms that our ancestors would never have dreamt about. Consequently, few of us have any experience of what submitting to the leadership of a king is like. We are used to our freedom and reluctant to lose it. Our fallen human nature so often wants to stay in control. To quote one phrase from a popular song, "I did it my way." We do not want to submit to the will of another and prefer the freedom to determine the course of our lives. Of course, God is a very good king and gives us complete freedom of choice: we can choose whether we will make Him Lord of our lives or not, but there will be ultimate consequences for the choices which we make, and we cannot expect His sovereignty and power to be manifested in our lives if we do not recognise and submit to His undisputed role as King over us.

In fact, complete freedom or independence is a fallacy. We often quote Paul's words in his letter to the Galatians: "It was for freedom that Christ set us free; therefore keep standing firm and do not be subject again to a yoke of slavery" (Galatians 5:1 NASB). However, Paul is speaking here about freedom from the Law. He goes on to say that if they submit to circumcision, they will need to obey the whole Law and will be alienated from Christ. When we are in Christ, we are set free from the rules and regulations of the Law. This is good news. However, freedom – written in this context – does not mean living independently. We were not created to live independently from God, and if we try to do so, we will find ourselves controlled by the world, the flesh and the devil – the forces who oppose us. We are deceived into believing that we are free to determine the course of our lives but we are just like puppets being controlled by the strings held by a puppet master.

This, I believe, is why so many of us continue to struggle with sin, even though we confess to have made Jesus our Lord and Saviour. Paul explains in his letter to the Romans, chapter 8, that it is when we are led by the Spirit that we are set free from the law of sin and death. When we try to live independently from God, we will be limited to our own strength and resources and will be no match against the spiritual forces of evil who wage war against us. It is only as we submit ourselves to God that we are empowered to resist evil.

Let us look at this truth in the form of a parable. If we consider the heavenly battle between good and evil, we – as a lone independent soldier – will be quickly annihilated by the forces of evil. However, if we enlist into God's army, and enlisting into any army always requires submitting to the authorities of that army, we will be surrounded, protected and empowered by God's far superior forces. This truth is confirmed in James 4:7 where he teaches us to submit ourselves to God before trying to resist the devil. It is only when we submit ourselves to God that the devil will obey our command to flee. It is only as we submit ourselves to God, that we are set free from the control of the world, the flesh and the devil.

The second reason why we may have failed to make Jesus our Lord is because we may not only read our Bible through the lens of our democratic culture but also through the distorted lens of our consumer culture as well. Most of us will have heard many presentations of the gospel and as evangelicals, we often pride ourselves on the purity of our understanding of the salvation message. However, if we go back to the New Testament – which must surely provide us with the most accurate account of the true gospel message – we find that Peter and Paul both preached a gospel message which had a very different focus to that of our twentieth- and twenty-first-century version, which has, in many cases, been affected by the consumer society in which we live.

If we look at New Testament passages where the gospel message is clearly presented, we find that Peter and Paul focused almost exclusively on the life, death, resurrection and exaltation of Jesus. In direct contrast, our presentation of the gospel is often focused on ourselves: on how our sins can be forgiven, our relationship with God restored and the promise of eternal life through Jesus' sacrificial death on the cross. This, of course, is all wonderfully true. However, if we present the gospel in this way, our focus is on ourselves and we have reduced Jesus to a commodity: the means through which we can receive all these blessing and benefits.

In this distortion of the gospel, we undermine the awesome majesty, glory, sovereignty and power of Jesus. Our focus is on ourselves and not on Him.

As a result, we lose sight of His unequalled ability to transform and empower our lives, robbing ourselves of the outworking of His power through us and limiting us to the little that we can achieve through our own efforts. If we have reduced Jesus to a commodity and have failed to make Him Lord in our lives, we will lack faith that He is sovereign over every situation which may concern us. The reason why the gospel message is such good news is that "Jesus is Lord". The four gospel accounts of His life show us that He is Lord (or sovereign) over all sickness, all disability, all evil spirits, all weather conditions and even over death. He is therefore sovereign over everything which controls us, troubles us and opposes us, and this would include our habitual sins and addictions. Distorting the gospel message in this way will deny us God's unlimited power to transform our lives and to make them fruitful.

The third reason why many of us may find it difficult to submit to the lordship of Jesus is based on our previous experience of being used and abused by significant people in our lives. Even in good relationships, we can sometimes feel as though others are taking advantage of us and we may have vowed never to allow anyone to have a position of power over us again. Furthermore, if we have loved someone who either rejected us or took advantage of our love and used it to exert power over us, we may have vowed never to fall in love again because we are afraid of further rejection, control or pain. It is also true that significant others may continually require something from us, and so we believe that we need to earn Jesus' love before He will pour His love and power into our lives. Let us remind ourselves of the wonderful truth that most of us know but few of us live by: God loves us just as we are, and Jesus died for us when we were still sinners. There is absolutely nothing that we can do which will cause Him to stop loving us and there is nothing that we can do which will cause Him to love us anymore.

We may be unaware of any deep feelings of hurt and insecurity within us, but they will, nevertheless, affect both our relationships with other people and our relationship with God. We may know in our head that Jesus loves us, but this wonderful life-changing truth may not yet have moved down to our heart where it will change our lives. It was some forty years after my conversion that a deep revelation of this truth of God's unconditional love for me changed me forever. Even if we do not remember making a vow not to fall in love again or to allow others to hold power over us, I would strongly recommend praying a prayer breaking any vow that we may have made. It is my understanding that meditating on the image of Jesus that is presented in the gospels will help us to know something of His beauty, majesty and faithfulness but a deep revelation of His great and unconditional love for us can only be received by direct revelation from God. To this end, we should ask God to reveal this awesome truth to us. It is probably the most significant life-changing gift that we can receive: a deep revelation of how much we are unconditionally loved and cherished by God regardless of what we may have done in the past or do in the future.

The fourth reason why we may have failed to make Jesus our Lord is because we have such a low opinion of ourselves that we do not believe that we are significant enough for God to have prepared a plan specifically for us or that He will lead us and guide us personally on a minute-by-minute basis. We disqualify ourselves without even asking God to reveal how special we are to Him or to lead us into a far more exciting and satisfying future. We think that because we are lacking in any personal value and ability, we will have to work out our own future and to serve Him through sheer hard work and self-effort. We often fail to recognise that so many biblical characters who were used very powerfully by God also lacked any self-confidence and God had to convince them that He would work wonderful miracles through them.

Let us look, for example, at the life of Gideon. First when the Angel of the Lord approached him, he disqualified himself by saying that his clan was the poorest in Manasseh and that he was the least in his father's house. Even after the Angel called him a mighty man of fearless courage and promised that the Lord was with him to give him victory, he still hesitated and asked the Angel to give him a sign that this message was indeed from God.

> Judges 6:11-18: "¹¹ The angel of the LORD came and sat down under the oak in Ophrah that belonged to Joash the Abiezrite, where his son Gideon was threshing wheat in a winepress to keep it from the Midianites. ¹² When the angel of the LORD appeared to Gideon, he said, 'The LORD is with you, mighty warrior.' ¹³ 'Pardon me, my lord,' Gideon replied, 'but if the LORD is with us, why has all this happened to us? Where are all his wonders that our ancestors told us about when they said, "Did not the LORD bring us up out of Egypt?" But now the LORD has abandoned us and given us into the

hand of Midian.' 14 The Lᴏʀᴅ turned to him and said, 'Go in the strength you have and save Israel out of Midian's hand. Am I not sending you?' 15 'Pardon me, my lord,' Gideon replied, 'but how can I save Israel? My clan is the weakest in Manasseh, and I am the least in my family.' 16 The Lᴏʀᴅ answered, 'I will be with you, and you will strike down all the Midianites, leaving none alive.' 17 Gideon replied, 'If now I have found favour in your eyes, give me a sign that it is really you talking to me. 18 Please do not go away until I come back and bring my offering and set it before you.' And the Lᴏʀᴅ said, 'I will wait until you return.'"

If this example of Gideon is not enough, let us remember Moses who said that he could not speak well, David who was over-looked by his father, Jeremiah who thought that he was too young, Rahab who was a prostitute, Joseph and Mary who were very poor, most of the disciples who were uneducated, Paul who had persecuted the church and, more recently, Mary Slessor and David Livingstone (missionaries in Africa) who both came from poor working-class backgrounds and Gladys Aylward (a missionary to China) who was rejected by the China Missionary Society, to mention just a few. The Bible makes it very clear that God chooses the poor, the downtrodden, the outcasts, the insignificant and the rejected and then transforms them and works through them to change history. God chooses "nobodies" and makes them "somebodies". Paul described this wonderful truth at the beginning of his first letter to the Corinthians. Let us meditate on this wonderful truth: our ability to serve God effectively and powerfully has absolutely nothing to do with our ability and everything to do with His ability.

1 Corinthians 1:26-31: "26 Brothers and sisters, think of what you were when you were called. Not many of you were wise by human standards; not many were influential; not many were of noble birth. 27 But God chose the foolish things of the world to shame the wise; God chose the weak things of the world to shame the strong. 28 God chose the lowly things of this world and the despised things – and the things that are not – to nullify the things that are, 29 so that no one may boast before him. 30 It is because of him that you are in Christ Jesus, who has become for us wisdom from God – that is, our righteousness, holiness and redemption. 31 Therefore, as it is written: 'Let the one who boasts boast in the Lord.'"

As I look back in amazement over the last forty years, I realise that there have been many challenges and choices which were to determine the wonderful opportunities and miracles that I have witnessed since. As I have already written in the previous chapter, I now recognise these challenges to be the keys which have unlocked the door to such an unexpected, exhilarating, and rewarding adventure. I also recognise that these different choices – although very different in nature – were all based on this one question: will I make Jesus Lord in this situation? Or to phrase this important question in a slightly different way: will I take the risk of giving myself to Christ, taking myself out of my keeping and putting myself into His keeping? I have taken this phrase from the Amplified translation of Paul and Silas' description of salvation. It is found in the passage where Paul and Silas have been thrown into prison but as they were praying and singing hymns of praise to God an earthquake shook the prison causing all the doors to be opened and all their shackles to be unfastened.

> Acts 16:29-31: "[29] Then [the jailer] called for lights and rushed in, and trembling *and* terrified he fell down before Paul and Silas. [30] And he brought them out [of the dungeon] and said, Men, what is it necessary for me to do that I may be saved? [31] And they answered, Believe in the Lord Jésus *Christ* [give yourself up to Him, take yourself out of your own keeping and entrust yourself into His keeping] and you will be saved, [and this applies both to] you and your household as well." (AMP)

If we consider this description of salvation as quoted above, the bracketed explanation in verse 31 has three distinct phrases: first, give yourself up to Him; second, take yourself out of your own keeping; and third, entrust yourself into His keeping. Each phrase of this explanation is important. We will find it difficult to submit to His lordship if we are still trying to keep ourselves because our resources are very limited, and we may well lack the necessary inner resources to cope with His more challenging directives. It is only when we take ourselves out of our own keeping and entrust ourselves into His keeping that we receive the power and ability to do whatever He asks of us because His resources are unlimited; and if He asks us to do something, He will always give us all the resources that we need to do it.

Jesus taught us that we should receive salvation as a little child. One reason for this is that the truth of the gospel is very simple – so simple that we, as adults, very often complicate it and miss the point completely. Let us consider Paul and Silas' above description of salvation, as translated in the Amplified version, in the form of a parable: I would like you to imagine that you are a child whose favourite toy has been broken. If you want your father to mend it for you, what do you need to do? Surely, all that is required is for you to place your toy into his hands and trust that he is both willing and able to fix it. In direct contrast, if you continue to hold onto it or give it to him only to take it back again, or if you keep interfering and telling him how he should fix it, he will not be able to respond to your request. We all know that such behaviour would be extremely foolish and yet we continue to treat God in a similar way. Surely, if we want God to heal our damaged and broken lives and to lead us into the abundant life that Jesus has promised us, we need to put ourselves entirely into His hands, stop trying to control our circumstances and to fix everything ourselves and allow Him the freedom to do whatever is necessary to achieve these two wonderful objectives.

Let us consider another example of this same principle: I would now ask you to imagine that you are ill and having visited your local doctor, he recommends surgery. Do you question his advice and refuse any treatment that he recommends? Surely you would not hesitate to yield your body entirely into the hands of the surgeon, in the sure knowledge that it is he who has the knowledge and experience to perform the necessary surgery and that you are not able to do it yourself. You will even allow the anaesthetist to put you to sleep, which must be the most vulnerable position that any human being can face because you will not even know what someone else is doing to you. So why, if we do not find it difficult to trust a doctor, an anaesthetist and a surgeon, who are only human beings like you and me, do we find it so difficult to trust God to heal our damaged and broken lives when it is He who both designed us and created us?

Surely, God knows better than anyone how to heal our shattered lives and to give us a future that overflows with His wonderful love, grace and power. However, if we are to benefit from His wisdom, power and skill, we need to place ourselves into His loving and competent hands and allow Him to act without interfering other than to thank Him in faith for the work that He is doing. How can He give us a positive future if we stubbornly hold onto control of our lives and refuse to do whatever He asks of us? Choosing to submit to His lordship and being prepared to do what He asks of us, will allow Him to transform our lives beyond anything that we could even dream about.

I find it helpful to use these parables and make them into a prayer. If I am facing a challenging situation, such as illness, danger, financial need or emotional pain, I pray a prayer of submission. One example would sound something like this: "Lord, You know that I am facing this worrying situation and I do not have either the physical resources to fix it or the emotional stability to cope with it. I therefore want to place myself into Your competent hands, trusting that You know exactly what needs to be done and have the power and ability to do it. I am choosing not to trust in my own very limited resources or to try to fix this situation in my own strength. I will trust Your advice and do whatever You ask of me. I believe that You can ultimately turn this situation around for good and I choose to leave this problem in Your hands except to obey any guidance and advice that You give me."

Let us draw this chapter to a conclusion by reviewing some practical ways through which we can finally resolve this issue of lordship. First, let us consider our independence for we will find it difficult to submit to the lordship of Jesus while we are still trying to keep ourselves and therefore limiting ourselves to our own resources. We need to act as the child with the broken toy and place ourselves into God's hands, declaring out in faith that we will no longer rely solely on our own resources but will instead trust in His unparalleled desire and ability to care for us. We need to check our hearts regularly to ensure that we maintain our dependence upon Him. We should thank Him every day in faith for His wonderful and unfailing love for us and continually look for signs of His presence and power working in our lives. We should not take anything for granted. The fact that we have air to breathe and food to eat is a sign of His love and care. We should thank Him for them. Recognising His presence in our lives in this way will build our ability to trust Him in every situation.

When we face difficult circumstances, we should continue to trust that He can bring good out of any bad situation. We need to look positively at our circumstances, even when they are difficult. God does not want us to be abused and never initiates pain or hardship, but He will sometimes allow difficulties which He can turn around for our benefit and to teach us of our need to depend on Him.

We need to learn to think biblically, and in faith. When we go through difficulties, we need to trust that God will provide all the resources – both physical and emotional – which will enable us to walk in victory through them. Even during difficulty, we should declare out our faith in God's presence and sovereign power, just like Paul and Silas when they were beaten and thrown into a dungeon. Instead of moaning and complaining about their circumstances, they prayed and sang hymns of praise to God. When they did so, an earthquake shook the prison so that all the doors were opened, and everyone's chains were unfastened. Maintaining a positive faith-filled attitude will enable God to work on our behalf.

When you have accustomed yourself to trusting in God's wonderful care for you, you can move on to the next step. Ask yourself if there is anything which you are not prepared to do for Him. This is likely to be something which frightens you, but it could simply be that of taking a humble servant-like role. Determine that you will overcome your anxiety, fear or lack of willingness to humble yourself, and strive to come to a place where you so value and desire a closer relationship with Jesus that you are prepared to do whatever is necessary to achieve this goal. We need to become like the man who found treasure in the field and was prepared to sell everything that he had to purchase the field, or the dealer of fine pearls who also sold everything that he had so that he could buy this one priceless pearl which he had found.

> Matthew 13:44-46: "[44] The kingdom of heaven is like treasure hidden in a field. When a man found it, he hid it again, and then in his joy went and sold all he had and bought that field. [45] Again, the kingdom of heaven is like a merchant looking for fine pearls. [46] When he found one of great value, he went away and sold everything he had and bought it."

It all rests on the value that we put on Jesus. When we discover something of His indescribable beauty, His wonderful faithfulness, His awesome power and sovereignty and the wonder and excitement of walking with Him, then we will see everything else as mere rubbish when compared with the sheer joy and thrill of walking with Him; we will be prepared to give and to risk everything to follow Him more closely and to know Him more intimately. We need to come to the point where our desire for Him is greater than our love for anything else. In my experience, as we begin to recognise His beauty, we will find ourselves thanking Him and seeking Him more; and as we do these two things, we will see even more of His unequalled beauty. In this way our desire for Him and the sense of His wonderful presence will grow and grow. This was Paul's experience. His relationship with Jesus was such that he was prepared to lose everything, and he considered everything that had been gain for him as rubbish when compared with the priceless privilege of becoming intimately acquainted with his beloved Lord and Saviour:

> Philippians 3:7-8, 10-11: "[7] But whatever were gains to me I now consider loss for the sake of Christ. [8] What is more, I consider everything a loss because of the surpassing worth of knowing Christ Jesus my Lord, for whose sake I have lost all things. I consider them garbage, that I may gain Christ . . . [10] I want to know Christ – yes, to know the power of his resurrection and participation in his sufferings, becoming like him in his death, [11] and so, somehow, attaining to the resurrection from the dead."

When our experience of and love for Jesus overshadows everything else, we will not find it difficult to submit to His lordship for we will be able to trust in Him completely and will be prepared to do anything to stay close to Him.

Chapter 3

"Follow Me"

Matthew 4:19: "'Come, follow me,' Jesus said, 'and I will send you out to fish for people.'"

Matthew 16:24: "Then Jesus said to his disciples, 'Whoever wants to be my disciple must deny themselves and take up their cross and follow me.'"

The wonderful simplicity and security of the gospel is summed up in the two words with which Jesus called His first disciples: "Follow Me." I believe that His call to each one of us is the same. Jesus makes it very clear that it is not for us to try to work out what we should do and where we should go. Neither is it for us to initiate the plans for our life. All we need to do is to follow Him and He will guide us and lead us into a life that is far more challenging and exciting than we could possibly work out for ourselves. He knows, far better than we do, where our gifting lies and which tasks we will find most satisfying.

It is therefore very clear that we will not be able to fulfil His plans for our life without Him. We were never created to live independently; we were created to live in dependence upon Him. Jesus described this partnership to be like two oxen yoked together, sharing the load. The wonderful truth is that when we follow Jesus, we are never alone, nor left to our own resources, nor asked to work out a solution to any problem which we face. When we follow Jesus, we work in partnership with Him and all His unlimited resources are available to us so that we can fulfil His plans and purposes for our life. It is therefore true that when we are yoked to Jesus, any difficulties which we face are light because we do not face them alone.

Matthew 11:28-30: "[28] 'Come to me, all you who are weary and burdened, and I will give you rest. [29] Take my yoke upon you and learn from me, for I am gentle and humble in heart, and you will find rest for your souls. [30] For my yoke is easy and my burden is light.'"

So how do we follow Him? First, we study the gospels so that we can learn from watching how He lived. To give just one example: when Jesus washed the disciples' feet, He said that He had given them an example which they should follow. The gospels are full of descriptions about how Jesus behaved in a whole variety of different circumstances and we are called to learn from Him and follow His example.

> John 13:12-15: "[12] When he had finished washing their feet, he put on his clothes and returned to his place. 'Do you understand what I have done for you?' he asked them. [13] 'You call me "Teacher" and "Lord", and rightly so, for that is what I am. [14] Now that I, your Lord and Teacher, have washed your feet, you also should wash one another's feet. [15] I have set you an example that you should do as I have done for you.'"

However, this alone will not be enough. If we are to follow Jesus, there are two further ways through which we are enabled to do this. First, it is essential for us to learn to hear and to recognise His voice speaking to us and this, like the building of any relationship, will take time and practice. Jesus said that His sheep will listen to His voice and follow His call:

> John 10:16: "I have other sheep that are not of this sheepfold. I must bring them also. They too will listen to my voice, and there shall be one flock and one shepherd."

Just as a new mother learns to recognise her own baby's voice from all the other babies lying in cots in a hospital, so we can also learn to recognise God's voice amid all the other voices which continually seek our attention. He can speak to us in a variety of different ways and these ways are likely to be different for each one of us. Sometimes, a verse in scripture will appear to leap off the page and we may receive an instant and new understanding of its meaning. For me, God often speaks through a clear word-by-word thought that comes suddenly into my mind. Together with any revelation there will also be an assurance in our heart that God has spoken to us. Of course, we need to test any word with scripture for He will never say anything that is contrary to His Word. We then need to choose to believe that He has spoken and obey Him even if it seems irrational and risky.

I still remember one wonderful way in which God spoke to me: I was in America when my mother's health deteriorated, and she was going in and out of a coma. Martin, my husband, phoned me with this news, and I flew home the following day. As far as I was aware, she was not a Christian, so I prayed desperately that she would be able to hear and to respond to the gospel message. As I was praying, this very clear thought came into my mind: "I will take her home." I knew that this was God because this phrase surprised me, and I knew that I would never have constructed a sentence in this way. When I got to the hospital, I was able to talk to her and to pray with her for salvation.

I cannot emphasise too strongly the importance of learning to hear God's voice. I am describing the ability to hear God say: "Sally, I would like you to do this and I would like you to do it this way!" Very often the way that we do something is even more important than what we do. God is outrageously humble, gracious, loving and generous and we are rarely any of these things, and so His way is usually very different from our own. Furthermore, God is committed to provide all the resources that we need to fulfil a plan that He has initiated, but He has absolutely no obligation to provide resources for our ideas, done our way!

Another advantage of listening to God speak to us is that it will give us faith to believe Him for the miraculous. Surely, if we have clearly heard God tell us what He plans to do, it is not difficult for us to believe that He will do it. In direct contrast, when we face a challenging situation and we receive no guidance from Him, how on earth can we possibly know how He will act?

However, if we are to hear God speaking to us, the issue of lordship must first be resolved. There are two reasons why surrender is essential if we are to learn to hear God speaking to us: the truth is that until we have decided that we will do whatever He asks of us, we will be fearful of listening to Him just in case He asks us to do something which we do not want to do. We have all experienced this truth in children. It is amazing how often they will pretend not to have heard us when we ask them to clean their rooms or to do their homework! If we want to hear God's voice, there must first be a strong desire to quieten our hearts, to give Him the opportunity to speak and then to believe that He has spoken, and we will be unlikely to do this if we are not prepared to do whatever He asks of us.

It is also true that God is not likely to speak to us if He knows that we are not willing to obey Him. This is, in fact, a sign of His mercy because we will be held responsible for something that we have heard but not obeyed. We cannot expect God to speak to us and then to be able to decide whether we will obey Him or not. No! We first need to decide that we will obey Him so that He will show us what He wants us to do.

Second, if we are to follow Jesus, we need to focus our attention on Him. We all know that if we want to reach an unknown location and a friend offers to lead us there, then we need to fix our eyes on him. If we take our eyes off him, even for a moment, *we* could take a wrong turn and get lost. Jesus called His disciples to follow Him because He knew that they needed to be shown the way. I personally do not believe that it is possible for us to discover the abundant life that He promises us without allowing Him to lead and guide us.

This advice sounds so simple, but it can be quite difficult to apply. As human beings we have such a strong tendency to be self-focused and in our busy lives there are so many distractions, all demanding our attention. Satan will also seek to deceive us and to distract us from following it. He does this in a variety of different ways. The first is through guilt. If he can get us to focus on our sin, then our eyes will be on self and not God. We need to remember that Jesus has paid the full price for our sin. If we sin, we need to repent and then trust that God has forgiven us and focus on His mercy. Our focus should not be on self, or confessed sin, but on God and His mercy.

The second way that Satan will seek to distract us is by constantly reminding us of those who have hurt us. If we give in to this temptation, this will not only take our attention off God, but we will become like those we look at. We see this truth in family life. Children learn from watching their parents and, as a result, often behave like them. The truth is that we become like those we look at and so if we fix our eyes on those who abuse us, we will become like them. In direct contrast, if we choose to fix our eyes on Jesus, we will become more and more like Him.

The third way we take our focus off God is through focusing on the problems that we face. You may remember how ten of the twelve scouts who Moses sent to investigate the Promised Land, focused their attention on the problems that they would face and all the reasons why they would fail to enter the Promised Land. When we do this, our eyes will be on our problems and not on the solution, and so we build our faith in these trials and undermine our faith in the awesome power and sovereignty of God to enable us to overcome in every situation.

In direct contrast, when we focus our attention on Jesus, on His awesome sovereignty and power, on the victory that He won for us on the cross, on the love and mercy that He continually extends to us, on the unlimited resources which are made available to us when we allow Him to lead and to guide us, on the fact that His everlasting arms uphold us and carry us when necessary, on the fact that He knows everything about us – both the good and the bad – and loves us unconditionally, then our lives will be transformed.

I have learned that surrendering to the lordship of Jesus, learning to recognise and choosing to obey His voice, and focusing our attention on Him, are the keys which will open the door to a new transformed, exciting and power-filled adventure where nothing within the confines of God's wonderful plan for our lives is unachievable. I believe with all my heart that God longs to demonstrate His love and care to a fallen world who desperately need a Saviour who will guide them into a more exciting, peaceful, fulfilling and fruitful future and that He is looking for channels – like you and me – to pour His love and power through. With all this in mind: how will you respond to His invitation to follow Him?

Chapter 4

Preparation and Testing

Deuteronomy 8:2: "Remember how the LORD your God led you all
the way in the wilderness these forty years, to humble and test you
in order to know what was in your heart, whether or not you
would keep his commands."

The first six years of my life as a new Christian were neither remarkable or exciting and consequently, I cannot remember much about this time. The fact that they were so mundane only goes to emphasise how unremarkable my life was before God stepped in to change it. However, it was during this time that God did ask me to take what turned out to be a few very significant steps and so I will share briefly what I remember of this time. The real adventure did not start until the beginning of 1984, but I am convinced that this adventure would never have happened without the preparatory steps of the previous six years. This, I believe, is also an important lesson for us: God is unlikely to lead us into an exciting adventure straightaway because He will first humble us and test us in preparation for what lies ahead. Just as the Israelites were humbled and tested in the wilderness, so God will take us through difficult, challenging, humbling or testing circumstances before He leads us into our own Promised Land.

Many books have been written which seek to teach us how we can see God's wonderful power working miraculously through us. However, in my limited experience, this kind of approach is often about self-promotion and self-effort and has little to do with giving God the freedom to act as He chooses through us. As I have already written in an earlier chapter, God's power is manifested in our lives when we place ourselves entirely in His hands and give Him the freedom to act in whatever way He sees to be appropriate and then obey whatever He tells us to do. Surely this was what the disciples did: they simply followed Jesus.

In considering these years of preparation and testing, I would like to look again at the story of Gideon. We find his story in Judges chapters 6 to 8. The event in Gideon's life that I want to focus on here is the well-known story of Gideon's army being reduced in size before they went into battle. You may remember that God had called Gideon to save his people from the hand of the Midianites who had been ravishing their land. The Israelite army initially numbered only 32,000 men. In contrast, the Bible tells us that the Midianite army was like locusts for multitude. However, God told Gideon that their army was too large for Him to give them victory lest they should boast that they had won the battle through their own efforts. He therefore instructed Gideon to send home all those who were fearful and 22,000 men left, leaving only 10,000. God then told Gideon that there were still too many men and that he should take them down to the water where God would test them.

> Judges 7:4-8: "⁴ But the LORD said to Gideon, 'There are still too many men. Take them down to the water, and I will thin them out for you there. If I say, "This one shall go with you," he shall go; but if I say, "This one shall not go with you," he shall not go.'
> ⁵ So Gideon took the men down to the water. There the LORD told him, 'Separate those who lap the water with their tongues as a dog laps from those who kneel down to drink.' ⁶ Three hundred of them drank from cupped hands, lapping like dogs. All the rest got down on their knees to drink. ⁷ The LORD said to Gideon, 'With the three hundred men that lapped I will save you and give the Midianites into your hands. Let all the others go home.' ⁸ So Gideon sent the rest of the Israelites home but kept the three hundred, who took over the provisions and trumpets of the others. Now the camp of Midian lay below him in the valley."

Before God used the Israelite army to defeat the Midianites, He tested them. God told Gideon that this was to be a test, but the Bible does not tell us that the army were informed and consequently they probably had no idea that the way they drank from the river would determine whether they would be involved in God's plan to rescue Israel from the Midianites. If God had told them that they were being tested, they may have changed the way that they drank, and it would not have been a genuine test. In a similar way, God is unlikely to tell us that we are being tested either. There was nothing dramatic or exciting about drinking from a river and there was nothing dramatic or exciting about my early years as a Christian. I could have so easily missed all the excitement that was to follow by failing to recognise and to obey the simplicity of God's first instructions because they did not appear to be either exciting or important. Although these early years do not make for very interesting reading, they were nevertheless essential as part of God's larger plan for my life. If, therefore, we are only looking for the extraordinary and sensational, we may miss the work that God is seeking to do in our lives.

If this example of Gideon's army is insufficient to convince us that God tests any man or woman before He promotes and empowers them, let us briefly remind ourselves that He tested Adam and Eve to find out whether they would eat from the forbidden tree of the knowledge of good and evil (Genesis 2:16-17), He tested Abraham to find out whether he loved Isaac more than Him (Genesis 22:1-20; Hebrews 11:17), He tested the Israelites to see whether they would obey His commands (Exodus 16:4; Deuteronomy 8:2, 16; Judges 2:21-22; Psalm 66:10; Isaiah 48:10; Hebrews 3:8) and He even tested Jesus in the wilderness at the very beginning of His ministry (Matthew 4:1; Luke 4:1-2). Surely, if God tested Jesus who is perfect in every way, then it is even more important for Him to test us BEFORE He promotes us and empowers us.

It is very possible that you may have already been tested by God and found to be lacking in some way. Like Gideon's army, you may have been unaware that God was testing you and thus you are now frustrated and perplexed as to why a door for ministry has not opened for you. You may have tried to fix this lack of direction by seeking to promote yourself. You may have served the church faithfully for many years and feel angry because your church leaders have not recognised your gifting or given you the opportunity to show your self-perceived worth and ability.

Let us remember that the Israelites' journey through the wilderness should only have taken eleven days. However, although the Bible records that all those who were numbered from twenty years old and upward who were able to go to war, were 603,550 – and this number would be far greater if men, women and children of all ages had been included in the census – only two reached the Promised Land. All the rest were found wanting during their time of testing and died in the wilderness. This is a stark warning for us. I am absolutely convinced that God has an individual plan, or a Promised Land, for every one of us which is just right for our personality and gifting, but we cannot enter it in our own strength, in just the same way as the Israelites were not able to conquer the land without God.

It is for God to promote us, not ourselves or other people. He may use others, but it will be through His motivating them to act on our behalf and not through our efforts to impress them or to earn recognition and honour. We may well have gifts that we are not even aware of, so how can we possibly expect someone else to know what they are? Only God can see deep into our hearts. He knows about every experience that we have faced, even those that we cannot remember! Even if our past has been abusive and painful, He is more than able to use all those experiences for good and to turn our life around completely. No experience, either good or bad, will be wasted. God never inflicts pain on us, but He will bring good out of our most painful experiences if we trust Him to do so. If, therefore, there is any possibility that we have been tested and found lacking, we should approach Him in humility and contrition, asking Him to give us a second opportunity and resolving within our hearts to be sensitive to His quietest whisper and to be prepared to obey whatever He asks us to do.

During the first six months after my conversion, it felt as if I was floating on a cloud of joy even though my circumstances had not changed. I also discovered that a few – but not all – of my fears had disappeared instantly, although I had to work through others many years later. It was during this time that there was considerable discussion about the infilling of the Holy Spirit and speaking in tongues, and so – not wishing to miss any of God's promised gifts – I sought and received this demonstration of the Holy Spirit's presence in my life.

Two years after my own conversion, my husband also discovered the blessing of a deeper walk with God. Martin had always been a far better church attender than I, and so it took him a little longer to recognise that he needed to take a far deeper step of commitment and trust. His conversion took place during a crusade that was being held at a local Youth with a Mission (YWAM) base. We had both been attending the local Anglican church but following

Martin's conversion, we decided to join the church that was started by YWAM after this crusade. This church was attended by several people who had been converted during the crusade, as Martin had been, and so there was a group of us who were all eager to learn as much as possible about our newly found faith. To this end, the church ran a "Disciples of Jesus" course which we both attended.

The church met in a newly constructed building in the grounds of Ifield Hall, the YWAM base in Crawley. It was an old and rambling house which needed significant repair. The main building was demolished some years later and the property sold to another charity. It was in this old building that the first of many tests took place, although I did not recognise it as a test at the time. We were members of the church located in the grounds of this YWAM base, but we had little to do with the operation of the mission which was being carried out in this large building. However, despite our lack of involvement with the activities within this building, I felt prompted to offer my support to the lady who managed the running of the house, offering to give one day each week to spring-cleaning the building on a room-by-room basis.

This building was not only old and dilapidated, but it also had high ceilings, and so it was quite difficult to clean and did not look very good even after working very hard on it. The actual work, therefore, was not very rewarding. I also need to add that housework was probably my most hated activity, but I felt so motivated by God to do this that I found it relatively enjoyable and we worked quite happily together on this job for several months before God spoke to me about undertaking a new venture which I will describe in a later chapter.

I did not give this episode in my life much thought at the time. As far as I was concerned, God had asked me to do something and I had done it as best as I was able. It did not seem to be either important, exciting or fruitful. There was certainly nothing clever or especially difficult about the task God had given me. It was only many years later when I came to understand some of the principles through which God operates, that I came to recognise its essential importance. So why was this seemingly unimportant step to do some housework so significant? We will consider this question in the next chapter.

Chapter 5

The Way Up is Down

1 Peter 5:6: "Humble yourselves, therefore, under God's mighty hand, that he may lift you up in due time."

When we read biblical stories of men and women who God promoted and used to change history, we often find that God allowed them to go through a process of quite extreme humbling first. Perhaps the best example of this is the story of Joseph but we also find this principle in the lives of David and Moses – to mention just two more – and even Jesus as well. Jesus, of course, did not need to humble Himself for He was perfect in every way. However, Paul described Jesus' steps in a downward direction very clearly:

> Philippians 2:5-11: "[5] In your relationships with one another, have the same mindset as Christ Jesus: [6] who, being in very nature God, did not consider equality with God something to be used to his own advantage; [7] rather, he made himself nothing by taking the very nature of a servant, being made in human likeness.
> [8] And being found in appearance as a man, he humbled himself by becoming obedient to death – even death on a cross! [9] Therefore God exalted him to the highest place and gave him the name that is above every name, [10] that at the name of Jesus every knee should bow, in heaven and on earth and under the earth, [11] and every tongue acknowledge that Jesus Christ is Lord, to the glory of God the Father."

I am convinced that if we want to be used by God to change history, one very significant key that will unlock the door to an exciting, fulfilling and fruitful ministry is humility. We have all seen worldly examples of men and women who have been promoted to places of authority and power only to abuse that position and to use it to inflict control, pain and abuse to those under them. There is the very well-known saying: "Power corrupts, and absolute power corrupts absolutely!" This is not the case in God's Kingdom. We find in the above description of Jesus that He never sought to promote Himself, but instead humbled Himself to the very lowest place, even to death on a cross. If, therefore, we want to be promoted to a place where we can achieve things for God, we first need to seek the lowest place and not the highest: in the Kingdom of God, the way up is down! Jesus made this principle very clear:

> Luke 14:7-11: "[7] When he noticed how the guests picked the places of honour at the table, he told them this parable: [8] 'When someone invites you to a wedding feast, do not take the place of honour, for a person more distinguished than you may have been invited. [9] If so, the host who invited both of you will come and say to you, "Give this person your seat." Then, humiliated, you will have to take the least important place. [10] But when you are invited, take the lowest place, so that when your host comes, he will say to you, "Friend, move up to a better place." Then you will be honoured in the presence of all the other guests. [11] For all those who exalt themselves will be humbled, and those who humble themselves will be exalted.'"

We need to consider Jesus' words very carefully. There is no ambiguity about this very significant warning: if we seek to promote ourselves and to take the glory that is rightfully due to God alone, then He will humble us. If, however, we choose to take a humble position and to serve without receiving any acknowledgement, reward or honour, then God will exalt us. If we want to be placed into a position where we can achieve great things for Him, then we need to seek the lowest place and not the highest! God has promised to exalt us but only on the condition that we do not seek to exalt ourselves.

I do not want to give you the false impression that doing some housework forty years ago was sufficient to fulfil this humbling process in my life. No, it was just the very beginning of a process that has continued in a variety of different ways right up to this present day. It is perhaps one significant sign that God is working in our lives: we will face a variety of different events and experiences which humble us and stop us from becoming proud and over self-confident. We find Paul describing how God continued to humble him in his second letter to the Corinthians:

> 2 Corinthians 12:7b: "Therefore, in order to keep me from becoming conceited, I was given a thorn in my flesh, a messenger of Satan, to torment me."

I am aware of at least two reasons why this humbling process is necessary. First, God can only enable us to achieve great things for Him when we trust in His ability and not our own. Our ability is extremely limited while His resources and power are unlimited. It is sadly true that pride can lead us to develop our own plans for ministry and to seek to promote ourselves because we have a false confidence in our abilities, and we are not prepared to pay the true cost of discipleship. Self-promotion and self-effort are completely unacceptable to God and will, in fact, stop Him from working on our behalf. As I explained in an earlier chapter, if a child holds on to his broken toy, his father will not be able to mend it; I was to learn this lesson in a challenging way a few years later. Humility, in direct contrast, will drive us to our knees and to recognise our dependence upon God. It is therefore necessary for God to bring us to a place where we recognise our own inability to achieve anything great through our own efforts and to come to a place where we have absolute faith and trust in Him, are willing to pay the true cost of discipleship and to depend on Him instead of ourselves. Jesus made it very clear that discipleship will be costly.

> Luke 14:25-33: "[25] Large crowds were travelling with Jesus, and turning to them he said: [26] 'If anyone comes to me and does not hate father and mother, wife and children, brothers and sisters – yes, even their own life – such a person cannot be my disciple. [27] And whoever does not carry their cross and follow me cannot be my disciple. [28] Suppose one of you wants to build a tower. Won't you first sit down and estimate the cost to see if you have enough money to complete it? [29] For if you lay the foundation and are not able to finish it, everyone who sees it will ridicule you, [30] saying, "This person began to build and wasn't able to finish."
> [31] Or suppose a king is about to go to war against another king. Won't he first sit down and consider whether he is able with ten thousand men to oppose the one coming against him with twenty thousand? [32] If he is not able, he will send a delegation while the other is still a long way off and will ask for terms of peace. [33] In the same way, those of you who do not give up everything you have cannot be my disciples.'"

Second, God will never promote a person who will take the glory that is rightfully due to Him alone. We find an example of this truth in the story of Gideon's army which we considered earlier: God reduced the number in the Israelite army lest they should boast that they had won this victory through their own efforts. When God works in our lives, it is through His power and not through our own, and it is therefore right that He receives all the honour and glory. Humble people will never draw attention to themselves but will instead continually focus their words and attention on God, giving Him all the glory for anything which they have been able to achieve.

If we consider the story of Joseph very briefly, we find that God ultimately exalted him to a position second only to Pharaoh. He also vindicated him in front of his father and brothers. However, prior to his vindication and exaltation were years of humiliation, false accusation and suffering. First, he was thrown into a pit by his brothers. He was then sold as a slave without any rights or possessions and taken to a foreign land – to a people he did not know and with whom he could not even communicate. Following this, he worked as a slave to Potiphar only to be falsely accused of rape by Potiphar's wife. He was then sent to prison where he remained for many years, even though he was completely innocent, before he was miraculously released. Throughout this time Joseph remained faithful to God and acted with absolute integrity. It would be easy for us to aspire to Joseph's exalted position but the question that we need to ask ourselves is this: are we prepared to pay the price that he paid to get there?

There is a well-known saying, "there's no gain without pain", and most of us will understand that we will not achieve success in any area of our lives without some cost or pain. Whether we are a businessman, a musician, an athlete, a doctor, a nurse or a church minster, we will not see success without some cost and/or pain. A musician will need to practise for hours each day and an athlete to do hours of training, which may require him to miss socialising with friends. An athlete will also need to discipline himself with what he eats. A nurse or doctor will require years of training and then costly commitment to their patients. A good pastor will need to spend hours caring for his congregation and reaching out to the community around him. However, we sometimes fail to apply this truth to our spiritual lives. In fact, this principle is even more true in our spiritual walk. Surely, if God is to work through us to change the course of history and to build His kingdom on earth, there must be a preparation period when He tests us to expose the true condition of our hearts and then moulds us into a vessel which He can use for His glory.

We can be envious of someone else with a successful business or a respected ministry in the church, but we need to recognise that it will have cost them some pain to get where they are. If we want their success or position, we will also need to pay a similar price as they did to get there. Many people want promotion, success, fruitfulness and honour but few are prepared to pay the price to achieve it. Real success in any venture in life will be costly. In my experience there is nothing that can even begin to compare with the awesome privilege and joy of walking with God and seeing Him work on our behalf, but there will be a price to pay. We may have looked for another less costly route. We may have even bought books written by Christian believers with a well-known and successful ministry in the false belief that we can learn how to achieve their success without experiencing their pain. However, the truth is that with God there is only one way and His way is narrow and costly!

> Matthew 7:13-14: "[13] Enter through the narrow gate. For wide is the gate and broad is the road that leads to destruction, and many enter through it. [14] But small is the gate and narrow the road that leads to life, and only a few find it."

> Matthew 16:24: "Then Jesus said to his disciples, 'Whoever wants to be my disciple must deny themselves and take up their cross and follow me.'"

Let us also consider the life of David: when God sent Samuel to anoint the next king of Israel, we find David shepherding his family's sheep. His father did not even consider him worthy of being presented to Samuel. Without the benefit of hindsight, it would be easy to expect his life to change for the better after Samuel had anointed him, but the reality was very different. Instead of David being elevated in preparation for his role as king, we find him being pursued by Saul like a common criminal. He was not only forced to live as an outcast, but even his life was in severe danger. Like Joseph before him, he chose to act with integrity despite the injustice done to him and refused to kill Saul even though he had the perfect opportunity to do so. Once again, we might aspire to David's position when he did become king, but would we be prepared to pay the price that he paid before God promoted him? Even after he became king, his troubles did not cease and his episode with Bathsheba shows that he was still vulnerable to sin.

Let us also remember that although Moses was bought up in a palace, he had to take refuge in the land of Midian where he spent nearly forty years as a simple shepherd. Even Gideon described himself as belonging to the poorest clan and being the least in his father's house. There are also brief references in the Bible to other people who were chosen by God and placed into a position where they changed history. Few details of their lives are recorded, but if we spend time considering their stories, we will find that they were humbled and even abused before they were promoted. Let us consider Sarah who suffered the humiliation of not being able to give Abraham a son and then watching her husband having a relationship and producing a son with Hagar.

There was also Tamar who was forced to marry Judah's wicked son, Er, and then suffered further humiliation when Judah's second son, Onan, prevented her conceiving a child because he knew that the first child would not be considered his, but would continue the line of his dead brother. Following this, she suffered the further injustice of Judah refusing to give her his third son, Selah, following Onan's death and according to the custom of the time. There was also Rahab who was reduced to prostitution before marrying Salmon and becoming part of the lineage of Jesus. Joseph and Mary were very poor for they were only able to offer a pair of turtledoves or two young pigeons when they went to Jerusalem to dedicate Jesus and most of the disciples were poor and probably uneducated fishermen. With many other biblical characters, we are not given any information about their lives before their public ministry began, but it is very likely they also went through a period of preparation even though it is not recorded in the Bible.

Let us draw this chapter to a conclusion by considering once again the amazing humility of Jesus. He did not only leave His place of glory and honour in heaven and take the lowest place of a common criminal on the cross, but He also took the place of the lowest servant and washed the disciples' feet, teaching us that we should follow His example. If we meditate on His example of humility and remind ourselves of the life-transforming benefits and blessings that we receive through His agonising and sacrificial death, we should find it comparatively easy to follow His example.

> John 13:14-15: "[14] Now that I, your Lord and Teacher, have washed your feet, you also should wash one another's feet. [15] I have set you an example that you should do as I have done for you."

Chapter 6

The Almond Tree

Jeremiah 29:13: "You will seek me and find me when you seek me
with all your heart."

The Youth with a Mission base in Crawley had the use of a local council-owned property in town where they had been running a pizza restaurant. This had closed recently and was lying vacant. After a few months of spring-cleaning in Ifield Hall, God spoke to me about opening this restaurant again. I discussed this with Martin and with our church leaders and, with their blessing and support, Martin and I started the work of preparing this building to serve a reasonably priced mid-morning cup of coffee or tea and lunch. The vision was to use this as an outreach facility and through it to build relationships within the Crawley community. We therefore spent some time redecorating the building and having the central heating overhauled. We also planted an almond tree in front of the building and named the restaurant "The Almond Tree". This name was to be a faith statement because the almond tree blossoms early in the spring.

Within a relatively short period of time the building was ready, and a group of church members offered to help us to run this restaurant on a voluntary basis. I remember that we used to meet to pray each morning before we opened, and this helped us to build strong and open relationships with each other and to sort out any difficulties before they disrupted the peace and unity that we enjoyed. This venture was very successful with several people who came on a regular basis. We were also able to build good relationships with many of our clients.

We also used to meet in this building on Friday evenings. A group of us would then go out into the town and invite people to come back for a cup of coffee or tea while the rest of us would stay in the building to pray and to serve the drinks for those who came back. I thought this would be a long-term commitment for Martin and myself, but it was not long before God revealed that He had other long-term plans in mind for us.

During this period, our only daughter, Ruth, was about ten years old and was attending a school near Billingshurst, a thirty-minute drive from our home. On one day a week when I was not working in The Almond Tree, I used to take her to school and then spend the day walking around the local area praying. I remember that there were several bluebell woods in this area which were a glorious sight in late spring, and it was such a joy to walk through them.

Although I cannot remember the general subject matter of my prayer-walks, I can remember one incident very clearly. I was walking towards the crest of a small hill when the thought came to me: if Jesus was suddenly to appear over the top of this hill, what would I do? Would I fall flat on my face? Would I just stand routed to the spot in sheer terror? Would I feel guilty or shy? What would I do? My whole focus was on myself and how I would react if such an awesome thing should happen. As I was pondering this question, it was as if the Holy Spirit took over my thinking and I saw in my mind a picture of Jesus – dressed in the conventional long white robe – coming towards me. As soon as He came into sight, He recognised me and, lifting the bottom of His robes, ran towards me. As He came nearer, He let go of His robes and opened His arms wide in greeting and welcome. It was such an unexpected and wonderful revelation of His love for every one of us and an indication of how special we are to Him that this memory has remained with me ever since.

I remember that I had a deep desire to draw closer to God and to learn more about Him. Although many aspects of my life were good, there was a deep longing in my heart for something more and I knew that I would only find this fulfilment through Him. The book that, more than anything else, developed my love for God at this time and my recognition that He is the source of all real joy and fulfilment was the autobiography of St Thérèse of Lisieux. I first heard about her on the children's programme *Blue Peter* where her life and the very dramatic effects of it were featured. Thérèse was a young girl who lived in Lisieux in north-western France towards the end of the nineteenth century and who became a Carmelite nun in her late teens. She had to get special permission from the Catholic authorities to join this convent at such an early age.

It would be almost impossible to exaggerate the profound and very positive impact that this book had on my life. I am so pleased that I read it very early in my Christian life as it formed the foundation of so much that was to follow and guided me, I believe, on a spiritual rather than a worldly path. Her writing revealed her passionate love for Jesus and the joy that filled her heart and life because of her very close relationship with Him. Because her focus was almost exclusively on Jesus and her love for Him, I believe that her writings can be appreciated by both Catholics and Protestants alike. I understand that since her death, the Carmel in Lisieux receive an average of sixty letters every day from people whose lives have been profoundly impacted by her and millions of copies of her autobiography have been sold in many different languages throughout the world.

I still remember one passage in which she describes so simply and yet so profoundly the wonderful way that Jesus' death transforms our lives. If I remember the passage correctly after over thirty-five years, she was thinking about the pathway to perfection and concluded that there was no way in which she could achieve perfection through her own efforts but wrote that she was not in any way downcast. She described how she saw the pathway to perfection like a staircase and that she was sitting at the bottom looking up at it when Jesus came down from the top and, picking her up in His arms, carried her to the very top.

There were two key qualities in her life which had a profound impact on me: first, her passionate love for God and, second, her humility – as the passage in the preceding paragraph shows. I still remember reading that she sought to demonstrate her love for God by performing small and very humble acts of love towards the other nuns and especially to those who had more difficult characters. Tragically, she caught TB while she was still very young and died when she was only twenty-four years old after a period of intense suffering. However, the positive impact that her very short life had on millions of people would be hard to overstate.

As a direct result of reading this autobiography, I started to go on three-day retreats in various convents where I could seek to develop the kind of relationship with God that Thérèse had enjoyed. Once again, I had discovered in her life something that I wanted desperately and was prepared to do almost anything to find for myself what she had found. I still remember the time that I spent in these convents and especially one enclosed order where they allowed two retreatants at a time to join them in the enclosed part of their building and to participate in convent life with them just as if we belonged to their order. In other convents the visitors' part of the building was separate to that where the nuns lived, although we could join them in their daily cycle of prayer – sometimes with a screen between us.

Another activity in which I was involved at this time and which was also to play a part in what was to come, was my membership of a Mother Teresa (of Calcutta) group who used to collect, prepare and pack clothing for India. It was the loving way in which this clothing was prepared by the group and the way Mother Teresa and her nuns poured their love and care on the very poorest outcasts in India that also had a very profound impact on me.

In drawing this short chapter to a conclusion, what becomes very clear to me is the amazing way in which God prepares us for the work that He has planned for us to do. He does not expect us to work it out for ourselves but brings people into our lives who will teach us all that we need to know. God knows all too well the pride, weakness, frailty and selfishness of our human nature and will give infinite care and attention to nurturing us and transforming us into a vessel whom He can use for His glory, if we will allow Him to do so.

It is also true that the closeness of our relationship with God will have a profound impact on our future ability to achieve anything of any significance for Him. Thérèse's life has resulted in thousands of people being drawn closer to God even though she never left the grounds of her convent after she had entered it. It must therefore have been the quality and fervency of her prayer-life and her very deep relationship with God which made her very short life so fruitful. She used to call herself "The Little Flower" and this name reminds me of John the Baptist's words:

John 3:30: "He must become greater; I must become less."

This statement should apply to every one of us: if we want Jesus to be more prominent in our lives, then we must become smaller or less prominent.

By smaller, I do not mean lacking in a sense of self-worth but quite the opposite. When we truly know how much we are loved and valued by God, we will stop seeking to promote ourselves and will instead delight in giving Him the glory for everything that we are enabled to achieve for Him. The less that we focus on and draw attention to ourselves, the more prominent Jesus will be in our lives.

Chapter 7

"I Was Naked"

Matthew 25:34-36: "[34] Then the King will say to those on His right, 'Come, you who are blessed of My Father, inherit the kingdom prepared for you from the foundation of the world. [35] For I was hungry, and you gave Me *something* to eat; I was thirsty, and you gave Me *something* to drink; I was a stranger, and you invited Me in; [36] naked, and you clothed Me; I was sick, and you visited Me; I was in prison, and you came to Me.'" (NASB)

Martin and I had met each other at Biggin Hill Airfield during 1970, where he was the chief flying instructor for one of the many flying schools there and I was one of his students. He was clearly a very good instructor because I gained my pilot's licence after the minimum number of hours required flying, even though my first instructor had absolutely no confidence in my ability to learn to fly and had therefore asked Martin, as the chief flying instructor, to teach me instead.

Towards the end of that year, Martin got a job flying as a commercial airline pilot and we got married in January 1971. We arranged the wedding after knowing each other for such a short period of time because Martin was told that they would be sending him to fly at one of their bases in the north of England and we wanted to get married before he left. However, just before the wedding he learned that a position had become available at Gatwick Airport and it was too late to delay the date of the wedding.

Towards the end of 1983, Martin felt led to take his one month's holiday and to ask for a further one month's unpaid leave during January and February of the following year – when the airline was less busy – and offer to work on a temporary basis for Mission Aviation Fellowship. MAF, a Christian charity, flies light aircraft which can land on small grass airfields to facilitate travel in countries where road travel can be time-consuming and difficult. This ministry is especially beneficial for medical emergencies but is also used by a variety of people who need to travel long distances from areas without good roads or commercial airports.

Having discussed this with his airline, we both went down to visit the head office of MAF in Ashford in Kent, only to discover that it would not be possible for Martin to fly for them for such a brief period because pilots had to be tested and registered in the country where they would be flying. However, when they discovered that he was also qualified and experienced as an aircraft engineer, he was asked if he would go to Dodoma in Tanzania where they were in desperate need of engineers.

Martin went to Dodoma in Tanzania for two months during January and February of 1984. I did not go with him during this first visit as our daughter was only twelve years old at that time and I did not believe that it was right to leave her, even if she were to stay with a friend. I therefore stayed at home with no idea of how this one visit would change our lives for ever!

Martin will testify that this was a life-changing experience. He stayed within the grounds of the Msalato Bible School which is located a few miles north of Dodoma. This compound was not only the base for the Bible school teachers and students but also for the international staff of the MAF base in this part of Tanzania. (MAF have more recently built their own compound nearer to their airstrip.) Martin therefore had the opportunity of not only building friendships with the MAF staff but also with several international teachers at the Bible School.

While he was in Tanzania, Martin worked in the aircraft hangar with other MAF engineers – both European and Tanzanian. One morning, one of his Tanzanian colleagues came to work dressed only in his trousers. In response to Martin's question about why he was dressed in this way, he explained that he had been burgled while he was asleep the previous night and that the burglar had taken virtually everything that he owned except for his trousers which he had put under his mattress to press for the following day. Martin felt challenged by this situation and decided to divide everything that he had with him in half and to give his Tanzanian colleague one half.

Martin was not only challenged by this one event, but he was also challenged by the general state of the clothing worn by many of the Tanzanian people at that time. Much of the clothing was in a very poor state. When his time came to leave, he gave all his clothing to Pam Wilding, one of the teachers at the Msalato Bible School where he had stayed and who was to become a very significant part of our work in the early years, so that she could distribute them as she felt appropriate. He came home with an empty suitcase.

International communication was not as easy and inexpensive then as it is now and so we did not communicate much while Martin was away, although I think that he did send me a few letters. I was not, therefore, aware of all that Martin had experienced. However, despite the limited communication between us, I was challenged by the many Bible passages which I read while he was away, teaching us that we should help those in need. When he returned with an empty suitcase and explained why he had left his clothing behind, we started to consider that God may be calling us to respond to this need that He had presented to us.

Knowing how impetuous I can be, I asked for confirmation that this was indeed God's leading and not just my good idea! Following this request, so many of my daily readings for the following six weeks included passages about our need to care for others. At the end of this period, I was totally convinced that God was indeed calling us to serve Him in this way. We learnt later how much we were to need this clear confirmation that this was God's plan for us to carry us through the testing time ahead.

I realised later that this chain of events was like Jesus' parable about the Good Samaritan. We cannot, as individuals, help everyone who is in need, but we can respond to the situations which God presents to us and these will be different for each one of us. It was as if God was saying to us: I have shown you this need, a need which you CAN do something about, and I am watching to see how you will respond.

What became immediately clear to me was the fact we, in the UK, had a significant surplus of the very items that were so badly needed in Tanzania. At that time, jumble sales were very much in vogue and most Saturdays there was a choice of several where clothing was piled two-feet high on long tables and most items only cost a few pence each. At most of these jumble sales there was so much clothing that much of it had to be taken to the local refuse facility afterwards. Added to this was the fact that my involvement in the Mother Teresa group had prepared me for just such a ministry.

During April and May, I therefore started to visit and to collect some very good-quality clothing from jumble sales. While I was doing this, God spoke very clearly to me and gave me three foundational principles which should guide this work which we had started. The first foundation principle was all about the importance of demonstrating love. God showed me that any clothing that we sent should be good quality and packed so that it looked like new: the guidance that came to my mind was that we should not send anything that we would not be happy to wear for best ourselves. I therefore only collected garments that were in good condition and suitable for the hot African climate. Each item was mended, if necessary, and then washed, ironed, sized and folded in the same way as you would find new garments folded in a shop. Each garment was then placed into a polythene bag, sealed and labelled with a description of the garment together with its size which was written in both Kiswahili and English.

I followed the example of the way the clothing had been so lovingly prepared and packed for India by the Mother Teresa group, but I also put each garment into a polythene bag to keep it clean and to enable me to label it with a description and the size of the garment. Each finished garment looked as if it was new, not second-hand. I did this on my own at home, and while I was preparing and packing the clothing, Martin packed the finished goods into tea-chests, labelled these tea-chests using a stencil showing the destination address, and tried to organise the transportation.

Months later, when our consignments had started to arrive in Africa, we received many letters from people saying that they had received God's love through the gifts that we had sent, and that they had been encouraged and strengthened in their service for God. Furthermore, by providing clothing, this ministry enabled individuals to receive God's love and care for them personally. Paul understood the essential value of love in Christian work:

1 Corinthians 13:1-3, 13: "[1] If I speak in the tongues of men or of angels, but do not have love, I am only a resounding gong or a clanging cymbal. [2] If I have the gift of prophecy and can fathom all mysteries and all knowledge, and if I have a faith that can move mountains, but do not have love, I am nothing. [3] If I give all I possess to the poor and give over my body to hardship that I may boast, but do not have love, I gain nothing... [13] And now these three remain: faith, hope and love. But the greatest of these is love."

This well-known passage on love teaches us that any practical work or sacrifice that is done without love has no value whatsoever. This is true. If our works of charity are not motivated by love, and instead elevate the benefactors while humiliating and degrading the recipients, the long-term results can be disastrous. It is essential that everything that we do is motivated by love and builds long-term self-respect in all those we are seeking to help.

Several years later, after we had started to send clothing to a lady who was ministering to children in Uganda, she told us that she had been so embarrassed when she had received some clothing from another organisation which included some urine-stained underpants. She had quietly burnt them before any of her Ugandan colleagues could see them. This is such a good example of performing some seemingly charitable ministry but one which humiliates the beneficiaries instead of communicating love and respect to them.

We have also benefitted in two ways from this emphasis on preparing the clothing with love: first, everyone involved in the packing of this clothing has found the work to be far more fulfilling and rewarding because the quality of the finished boxes gives a much greater sense of satisfaction. Second, as we have given out love to others, we have received a further infilling of God's love for ourselves. I have learnt over many years that as we minister love to others, we ourselves are increasingly filled with love and joy.

The second foundational principle was all about the growth of our ministry. The biblical story which came to my mind was the Feeding of the Five Thousand. This story gave me a conditional promise and a very clear picture of God's role and my role in this work. When we step out to minister for God,

I believe that we often make two significant mistakes: we either do all the work ourselves and leave God completely out of the picture or we fail to do anything until we see God perform for us. My understanding is that we should work in partnership with Him: when we play our part, God will work alongside us. Sometimes it is a case of us doing what we CAN do and leaving God to do all that we CANNOT do.

As I read that biblical story, I believe that God asked me to act like the small boy and to give what I had. However, He also made it very clear that it was His role to multiply my efforts. I should not therefore seek to multiply our work by asking anyone to help me or to advertise what I was doing in any way. He promised that on the condition that I did not try to multiply the work myself, He would do this for us. As I continue to tell the story in future chapters, I believe that you will see the amazing way that God honoured this promise. Many years later, I can testify that He has not only multiplied the work of packing clothing beyond anything that we could have even dreamt of, but He also used this work as a platform from which to develop a variety of other ministries as well. This is a further lesson that I learnt: we should work in partnership with God. Also, as we humbled ourselves and washed and ironed clothing for others, God later opened doors into a whole variety of other amazing ministries.

The third and last principle which God gave me at this time was all about the sensitive subject of money. This is an issue with which so many of us struggle and where we often lack a clear understanding of biblical principles. I had started to pack clothing for Tanzania, and we were immediately faced with the question of how we were going to fund the transportation of these boxes. With Martin's link with the airline business, we did consider that we may be able to apply for some free transportation on a space-available basis. However, as I was considering this, I believe that God spoke very clearly, and in fact reprimanded me for my thoughts on this subject. He said: Am I not able to provide the necessary funds for the transportation, do I not own the cattle on a thousand hills, and would it glorify Me if you were to go scrounging for money or free transport from different non-Christian organisations?

I immediately considered how I would feel if our daughter, Ruth, was to go around asking other families for money and how that would make us look as parents who were not able to provide for her. God went on to promise that, on the condition that we never asked for money or advertised our need for finances, He would provide everything that we needed. Thirty-three years later I can testify that we have kept our side of this request and that we have never had a bill which we did not have the funds to pay for.

Upon further reflection later, I realise the enormous significance of these second two principles for they led us to trust entirely on God rather than ourselves, and thus enabled God to do what would have been impossible for us to do without Him. I am absolutely convinced that if we had not stepped out in faith in this way, our work would never have amounted to anything significant and would probably have ended many years ago.

About two weeks after God had spoken to me about not asking for money, and at a time when almost nobody knew what we had started to do, we received an envelope containing £20 in cash with a note on the envelope saying: "For sending clothing to Africa." What a wonderful confirmation that God would honour His side of this agreement. To date, we still do not know who gave us this wonderful and very encouraging gift.

A few days later we received two more cheques for us personally and we knew that we needed to give these to the work as well. The Lord asked us to open a bank account so that He could continue to provide finances for this work. He also showed us that the name of the bank account and the work that we had started should be called "Faith in Action" from James 2:14-17 in which James clearly confirms that if we claim to have faith, then there needs to be action which demonstrates this.

> James 2:14-17: "[14] What good is it, my brothers and sisters,
> if someone claims to have faith but has no deeds? Can such faith
> save them? [15] Suppose a brother or a sister is without clothes and
> daily food. [16] If one of you says to them, 'Go in peace; keep warm
> and well fed,' but does nothing about their physical needs,
> what good is it? [17] In the same way, faith by itself, if it is not
> accompanied by action, is dead."

Many people wrongly believe that James is implying that our salvation is earned by our good works, rather than a gift received by faith. I believe James is saying that if we have received salvation, and thus God – Who is love – dwells within us (Galatians 2:20), then there will be outer demonstration of His inner presence through our actions. Consequently, if there is no outer demonstration of His inner presence, we should ask ourselves whether God truly dwells within us.

Chapter 8

The Name Above Every Name

Philippians 2:9-11: "[9] Therefore God exalted him to the
highest place and gave him the name that is above every name,
[10] that at the name of Jesus every knee should bow, in heaven and
on earth and under the earth, [11] and every tongue acknowledge
that Jesus Christ is Lord, to the glory of God the Father."

Even though God had faithfully provided finances for the transportation of
the goods that I had packed, by the following August we had come to a point
of almost total despair as nothing had arrived safely. It was very hard to
continue with all the work involved in the collecting, preparing and packing
of the clothing without seeing any positive results. However, we knew that
God had spoken and that somehow, sometime, He would sort everything out.

It was only this strong conviction that God had called us to do this work
that gave us the motivation and the faith to continue. It is for this reason
that it is so important for us to know what God has called us to do. If our
ministry has been initiated by Him, we can be assured that He will resolve
any difficulties that we face. In direct contrast, He has no obligation to
resolve any problems or obstacles that we face when we are only acting
according to our "good ideas"!

Following the loss of our first consignments, the thought came to me that I
should add a greeting onto each clothing label saying: "We send greetings in
the name of the Lord Jesus Christ." There are two reasons for this: first, it is
culturally appropriate in Africa to bring or to send greetings to everyone.
Second, and perhaps even more importantly, it clarified the focus of our
ministry and hopefully exalted the name of Jesus through the quality of our
clothing. This greeting was written in Kiswahili which is the language spoken
in Tanzania. Shortly after this, boxes started to arrive safely in Tanzania.
We have continued to include this greeting in the appropriate local language

on all our clothing labels and very few boxes have got lost over the past thirty-three years since we made this change. I have learnt since that God sometimes allows delays and opposition to test our faith and commitment and to see if we will continue to trust Him even when our efforts seem ineffective.

Over recent years I have also learned an even more significant lesson: there is great spiritual power in the name of Jesus. Each time that we have exalted His name and worshipped Him, we have seen awesome and wonderful things happen. When we focus our attention on Him and boldly exalt His name and worship Him, regardless of whether we see any visible sign of His presence or victory, the power of satanic forces is overcome and defeated.

It was five years after we started to include Jesus' name on every garment label and two years after I had started to travel more extensively around East Africa that I witnessed a miraculous and tangible demonstration of this wonderful truth: I was travelling around Uganda with the pastor of the church which we attended in the UK. During this trip we spent a few days travelling with each of the leaders of the churches with which we were working in this country. On our final day with one of these leaders, we visited a location where his church had been holding an outreach crusade. It was Saturday evening and they had held this evangelistic event each evening that week. The leader with whom we had been travelling approached some of his colleagues to ask how successful this outreach had been. Their reply was very negative. Apparently, this was an area which was known to be resistant to the gospel, not many had attended their meetings and even fewer had responded positively to their message.

There was only a small number of people gathered in that location that evening. The church leader with whom we had been travelling told his colleagues that he would preach. His message focused exclusively on some of the awesome truths about Jesus. He spoke His name in virtually every sentence. Everything he said glorified and exalted Jesus. I was listening intently to his words when, about half way through his message, I literally heard what sounded like a clap of thunder. Soon after this people started to join us, and the number steadily increased until there was a large crowd all standing around the raised stage on which this leader was standing.

When he finished his message and called for those who wanted to receive salvation to come forward, most of that large crowd surged forward.

I will never forget that evening. Before my eyes had been a very tangible demonstration of the awesome power and sovereignty of Jesus. When we make Jesus our Lord and Saviour and focus our attention on Him, declaring out the truth of His exaltation, victory and glory, the powers of evil are overcome. I believe that the clap of thunder which I heard marked the moment in time when the evil powers which had held this area in bondage for so many years were broken by the awesome and wonderful power of our Lord and Saviour.

I have also witnessed many other examples of this wonderful truth. Let me mention just two more. It was about the same time as I started to pack clothing that Martin woke up at about 2am one morning to see flames lighting up the sky outside our house. Upon closer investigation, he saw that his motorbike, which he had parked about six feet from our house, had been set on fire. Fortunately, a neighbour had already seen the flames and had phoned the fire brigade who arrived quickly at the scene. We found later, when the fire had been put out, that the fuel pipe of the motorbike had been cut so that the fuel had poured onto the ground. This was then set alight and the fire had been so hot that the motorbike had almost completely melted except for a few "Jesus stickers" which our daughter had bought and stuck on the front and back mud-guards. Even though the metal had melted in the heat, these paper stickers and a small area around them had only been singed but not burnt! We could still read the word "Jesus" on every sticker. I realise that this story will sound incredible, but I have learnt never to exaggerate the truth of what I experience as a lie is never glorifying to God and He does not need our exaggeration!

We saw another example many years later in Malawi. A plague of fall armyworm devasted crops throughout many countries in southern Africa in 2016 and the situation had been especially bad in an area called the Lower Shire in Malawi where we were working with a very large group of churches. We were told that communities in that area had lost 70 per cent of their crops. We did provide funds for sprayers and pesticide to combat this pest, but the crops needed regular spraying to stop the worm re-invading the land from neighbouring fields and it would have been extremely expensive for us to provide this protection for all the communities where we were working.

The following year, we strongly recommended that church members should go out into the fields to praise and exalt the name of Jesus and many of them did this each Sunday afternoon after the church meeting in the morning. We heard later that although there had been reports of this fall armyworm throughout southern Africa during that year, and this included many areas in Malawi, there was no sign of them in the fields where churches had exalted the name of Jesus in a committed and regular way.

In drawing this brief chapter to a conclusion, let us reflect again on our strong tendency to focus on ourselves. Much of it can appear harmless and can give a false image of contrition and humility. We think that we are not worthy of God's presence and blessing; we focus on our mistakes and confessed sin or we struggle to perfect ourselves and to perform impressive tasks for Him. However, through doing this, we undermine the awesome depths of God's mercy and the life-transforming power of Jesus' death on the cross, and through doing so, we deny ourselves access to the power and victory that God wants to pour into our lives. I am convinced that everything will change when we take our focus off ourselves and fix our attention firmly on our wonderful and gracious Lord and Saviour.

Chapter 9

It is God Who Multiplies

Isaiah 55:8-9: "[8] 'For my thoughts are not your thoughts, neither
are your ways my ways,' declares the LORD. [9] 'As the heavens are
higher than the earth, so are my ways higher than your ways and
my thoughts than your thoughts.'"

Hudson Taylor, the well-known missionary to China, is reported to have said: "God's work, done God's way, never lacks God's supplies." I have found that the way in which we do something is often more important than what we do. As I have already written in an earlier chapter, it is perfectly possible to perform some seemingly charitable task, but it is done in a way that elevates self while humiliating the beneficiaries. This is not God's way! In my experience, God's guidance nearly always includes quite detailed instructions about the way in which He wants me to perform the various tasks that He gives me. I was soon to learn how very important it is to follow God's instructions in every detail.

I continued to work at the coffee shop for three days each week while at the same time collecting, preparing and packing clothing on my own at home. We were committed to obey God's guidance and not to ask anyone to help us in this work nor to ask for any finances. By September of 1984, some boxes had started to arrive safely in Tanzania. It was during this time that God confirmed His promise that He would multiply the work which we had started. I thought, therefore, that I should resign from working at the coffee shop so that I could spend more time packing clothing.

However, following the departure of several members of the coffee shop team, God asked me to work there full-time for as long as they needed me. I cannot adequately describe how much I struggled to obey this directive as it seemed completely contrary to all that He had promised about multiplication and my focus and interest was now in the collecting and packing of clothing. However, I knew that God had spoken and after a short time of intense inner struggle, I offered to work full-time in the coffee shop.

For the next three months, the work of packing clothing decreased and instead of multiplying our new ministry, it almost came to a halt. This appeared, at the time, to be a significant step backwards but I have learned since that God's ways are not our ways and that it is sometimes necessary to lay all our efforts on the altar, just as Abraham was prepared to do with Isaac. Before I laid this work down it was still being achieved in my own strength, but afterwards I found that it was anointed and enabled with God's strength.

Following a short time of testing and frustration, two wonderful and miraculous things happened during December of this first year: first, another person offered to work as manager of the coffee shop, and I felt that God was releasing me to stop working there. Second, our church leaders asked Martin and me to lead a mercy group within the church and so a group of us started to meet one evening each week to pack clothing. This led to a significant increase in the amount of packed clothing. God is so faithful when we obey Him instead of following our own plans.

I understood later how significant this test was. If I had resigned from the coffee shop when I had planned to do this so that I could pack more clothing, then the growth of the work would have been limited to what I could do – which would be extremely limited. By asking me to work full-time in the coffee shop, God was making it almost impossible for me to multiply the work through my own efforts. Through obeying His instructions, I was placing the multiplication into His hands and He almost immediately provided a team of about eight other people to work with us. If we are to see God make our work for Him fruitful, our trust must be in Him and not in ourselves. As I continue to tell the story, you will see that He continued to multiply the work in ways beyond our imagination.

Martin and I both visited Tanzania at the beginning of the following year. After our return at the end of February 1985, we started packing as a church group. Instead of working alone at home, we asked members of the group to wash, iron and size the clothing at home during the week and then we all met together one evening each week to pack the clothing which had been prepared. We set up a long table in one of our houses and formed a packing line where the prepared clothing was passed from one end of the table to the other. Each garment was first placed into a polythene bag and then sealed, labelled, placed in a box and listed on a document list.

I well remember one couple who used to come together. There were occasions when the husband, upon recognising one or two of his shirts being passed down the line, all washed, sized and folded ready for packing, exclaimed in horror, "That looks like my shirt!" His wife had decided to give away those shirts which she thought he no longer needed without asking him. I am pleased to say that he always graciously accepted this loss without any argument, but I still remember the surprised and shocked look on his face.

Everyone involved in our packing group really enjoyed both the work and the fellowship that we had together. Because we had established a system for packing the clothing, we were able to talk as we worked. Our boxes continued to arrive safely in Tanzania and as the work increased so the finances increased as well, even though we never asked for support or even made our need for funds for transport known.

During June, I returned to Tanzania together with two members of our packing group. In fact, it was the couple whose husband had relinquished several of his shirts! While we were in Tanzania, I felt strongly from what we learnt there that we should start to transport our consignments in shipping containers instead of tea-chests. I discussed this with Martin upon our return and we telephoned a shipping agent to ask for a quote for transporting a 20-foot container consignment to Dar es Salaam. They quoted a figure of about £1,000 for the shipping costs which we immediately realised would be far cheaper than sending smaller consignments. We also realised that it would be far more secure to transport our boxes in a sealed container. Amazingly, the shipping agent asked us if we would like a shipping container which they provided one month later completely free of charge and without our even asking!

We both felt that this was wonderful confirmation that it was right for us to take this step of faith and so we started to pack into shipping containers, which no longer had a certificate of seaworthiness, as stores in which to keep our finished boxes which were waiting for transportation. Following the free provision of this container, we have had to pay between £440-£800 for their purchase. (The advantage of using a shipping container as a store meant that we knew when we had enough boxes to transport.)

The free shipping container which we had been offered was delivered to a site adjacent to The Almond Tree Coffee Shop and we started to put boxes into it. We were amazed at its size and were very concerned at how insignificant our boxes looked each time we put them in. We wondered whether we would ever fill it! It measured 20 feet by 8 feet by 8 feet and we calculated later that it would hold about 20,000 garments. Since then, we have sent 133 20-foot container consignments to five different countries in East Africa and several smaller consignments as well. As each container holds about 616 apple boxes, this total amounts to about 81,300 or between 4 to 5 million garments all packed with care and love!

It was at this time that another wonderful thing happened: as our consignments continued to arrive safely, some missionaries in Tanzania, seeing the standard of our clothing, wrote to their link churches back in the UK telling them about our work. It was the quality of our clothing which especially drew their attention as it was so different from goods that they had received from other donors. We started to receive telephone calls from people in churches whom we did not know, asking if we could come and show them how to set up a packing group in their church. Different churches continued to contact us. Some of them did so because they had missionary links in Africa, others had friends in a church who were already packing with us. Within eleven years, we had started ninety-two packing groups in churches of different denominations throughout the UK. I would emphasise that all churches contacted us, we did not contact any of them, and in fact we did not even know any of them before they contacted us.

During these early years, I spent a great deal of time driving around the UK, visiting and speaking in the various churches who had contacted us and showing them how to set up a packing group. I also prepared a manual with all the instructions, translations and necessary information needed to set up a packing group and provided these for each group who joined us. This enabled every group to pack to the same standard and conformity, making it easier for us to co-ordinate the transportation of the finished consignments.

Upon Martin's return from his third trip to Tanzania in February 1986, our first container consignment was full and ready to leave. It contained approximately 10,000 articles of clothing, all washed, ironed and packed with love, and many other items such as blankets, sheets, shoes, soap and sewing materials, etc. and it arrived safely in Dodoma during May that year.

Following God's promise to multiply our work, He not only moved within the hearts of so many wonderful people within a variety of different churches in the UK, but He also set up links for us within churches in the United States, Denmark, Malawi, Burundi, Uganda, Zambia, Rwanda, Mozambique and South Africa. Let me bring this chapter to a conclusion by giving a little more detail of this multiplication and explain how some of these links came about. I would emphasise, once again, that we did nothing to initiate any of this wonderful growth. I will share more in the following chapter.

First, let me share some brief details about the growth that we saw in the UK. We set up eight church-based packing groups during 1986, seventeen new groups during 1987, eight new groups in 1988, ten new groups in 1989, seven new groups in 1990, eleven new groups during 1991, seven new groups in 1992, twelve new groups in 1993, six new groups in 1994, five new groups in 1995 and one further group in 1997, making a total of ninety-two packing groups throughout the UK in a period of eleven years. I should add that all this growth happened before the internet was used widely as it is today!

Additional to the wonderful growth that we saw in the UK, God also set up links for us in the United States and Denmark. I was invited to spend ten days in Easton, Pennsylvania during April 1988 because a group of churches there wanted to set up groups packing for Uganda. Members of these churches had heard about our ministry from Michael Kajumba Walugembe, a Ugandan who we had met briefly when he passed through London on route to America. During this trip, I was able to speak with a number of churches in Easton and by the end of this brief visit, six groups were ready and anxious to start.

The following year, we received a letter from Jack Kinneer, pastor of the New Life Presbyterian Church in Pennsylvania who had offered to co-ordinate their consignments to Uganda, saying that he had visited Uganda during January and had had a very successful and encouraging time. They had contacted many churches and were hoping to complete their first container consignment of clothing during that year. They had also started an orphanage for seventy children on thirty-five acres of land given to them by the government and he testified of God's blessing as they had stepped out on this venture, informing us that their mission budget had increased from $2,000 to $18,000 and even their local operating budget had increased by about $8,000 during the previous year.

During October 1988, I was invited to visit Denmark. Flemming and Marryann Kjaer had heard about our ministry and wanted to set up packing groups in Denmark which would support some work they planned to do in the shanty towns in Bogota, Columbia. I spent a very encouraging and successful time with them, as a family, and was able to meet with people who were interested in supporting their planned ministry in South America.

Towards the end of 1987, David Kaczmarski came to England from America to pastor the Horringer Court Christian Fellowship in Bury St Edmunds. We had set up a packing group in this church before David came to England. Following his meeting with Lameck Msamange and Peter Guta in May 1988, when we visited several of our packing groups in the UK, David visited Malawi on several occasions but later returned to America to spend more time with his elderly parents. Once he was settled into his new church in Torch, Ohio, he invited me to visit their church so that they could start a packing group packing for Mozambique.

I spent a week in Ohio, USA, during February 1993 and was so encouraged by the love and welcome that was extended to me by all the members of the Torch Baptist Church. They also showed tremendous interest in everything that I shared with them and have since been able to pack two 20-foot container consignments for Mozambique. After several years of faithful packing, they decided to stop packing for Mozambique but to continue packing for a more local charity as the cost of transporting consignments from America to Mozambique was very expensive.

While we were building the number of packing groups in the UK, we were also, at the same time, building links with different churches in East Africa and setting up a different container store for each new destination. I will share about the growth of our church links in Africa in later chapters.

During the following six years, we set up container stores in Crawley, Handcross, Bedford, Hemel Hempstead, Huddersfield, Plymouth, Loughborough and Garforth, and different church groups co-ordinated our consignments to ten different locations in five different countries in East Africa.

The setting-up of our container store in Plymouth happened in an especially encouraging way. I contacted Percy and Margaret Lamerton in Plymouth during August 1990 to ask whether they would be interested in co-ordinating our consignments to Burundi. They said that they would like to come and discuss the matter with us, and we arranged a date later that month.

At 4pm, on the same day as I had this telephone conversation with Percy and Margaret, I received a telephone call from David Ndaruhutse, who would co-ordinate these consignments in Burundi, saying that he was on a visit to England and would be in our area during the same week that we had just arranged for Percy and Margaret to visit us. I was therefore able to arrange for David to come on the same day so that we could all discuss the matter together. Percy and Margaret could hardly believe the story when I shared it with them and felt convinced that this was God's confirmation to them that they should take on this new responsibility. Since that day, Percy and Margaret have been able to build a strong friendship with David which has made their work far more meaningful and he, together with several of his colleagues from Burundi and Rwanda, have stayed with them on their various trips to England.

As I look back on this part of the story, I remain amazed and overwhelmed by the wonderful goodness and faithfulness of God. How foolish we are to deny ourselves the wonder and excitement of working with Him when we trust in our own ability to serve Him and do not, at the same time, trust Him to work with us.

Chapter 10

Travelling in East Africa

Exodus 23:20: "See, I am sending an angel ahead of you to guard you along the way and to bring you to the place I have prepared."

Deuteronomy 1:32-33: "[32] In spite of this, you did not trust in the LORD your God, [33] who went ahead of you on your journey, in fire by night and in a cloud by day, to search out places for you to camp and to show you the way you should go."

Following Martin's first visit to Tanzania at the beginning of 1984, he spent another two months with MAF in Tanzania at the beginning of 1985 and again in 1986. On the second two occasions, I joined him for two weeks: two weeks that radically changed my life. I was deeply challenged by the simplicity and warmth of the African lifestyle and their commitment to evangelism. I was also encouraged by their deep gratitude for the work that we had started. My resolve to support them was increased a hundred-fold. It was during my second visit to Tanzania during the summer of 1985 that we felt led to start packing in 20-foot shipping containers instead of tea-chests.

Following these early visits to Tanzania, I started to travel quite extensively round different countries in East Africa. I was in the very fortunate position of being able to get 10 per cent stand-by tickets through Martin's position as an airline pilot. Miraculously, throughout the many years that I was able to travel in this way, there was only one occasion when I did not get onto my planned flight, and on this one occasion I got onto the flight the following day and, as circumstances turned out, this was a much better option for me.

Our first link was with the Anglican Diocese of Tanganyika, based in Dodoma, through our staying in the compound of the Msalata Bible School which they shared with MAF. Through our link with this church, we began to make contacts with another Anglican diocese in Tanzania. In 1986, I met Bishop Dudley Mageni from the Diocese of Morogoro and in 1987, I met Bishop Gershom

Nyaronga from the Diocese of Mara while he was visiting Dodoma. In the same year, we also contacted the Anglican Diocese of Victoria Nyanza through some missionaries who worked there and the Kanisa La Pentekoste based in Dar es Salaam through Phanuel and Siyuni Shikihiyo – who we met in Leeds.

In 1989 – shortly after the new Diocese of Tabora was formed – we met Bishop Francis Ntiruka in Dodoma, and when the Assistant Bishop of Central Diocese of Tanganyika – Bishop Donald Mtetemela – became Bishop of the new Diocese of Iringa, we continued our friendship with him in this new diocese. We also started to pack boxes for the Pentecostal Holiness Church in Iringa through some contacts that we made in the UK. By the end of 1989, we were packing consignments for all these churches in Tanzania and I had visited every church except for the Anglican Diocese of Tabora. Wherever I went, I was welcomed very warmly and enjoyed the very generous hospitality which is so much part of the African culture.

There is so much that I could write about my travels in Tanzania. My time there was especially memorable as it was the first African country that I visited – except for passing briefly through Nairobi. The scenery is so vast and flat; the African culture is so warm, gracious, generous and friendly; life is so vibrant, and far less pressurised; the colours everywhere – including clothing, flowers and birds – are so bright; and there is a wonderful openness and interest in the gospel.

The one experience that I perhaps remember best was the overnight bus journey from Dar es Salaam to Dodoma. For the Westerner, it was a long journey lacking any toilet facilities. (I am sure that local people knew exactly where many of these were located but if you are travelling alone with a large suitcase, it is difficult to get off the bus and trust that no one will steal it.) I therefore made a point of not drinking much for the day before we left. At each town where we stopped briefly, there would be lines of street vendors all cooking food by candle-light along both sides of the road and all anxious to make a sale to the passengers of each passing bus, most sales being passed through the windows. It is hard to adequately describe the vibrancy of the scene. It is one of those situations where you need to experience it for yourself and no words alone could accurately do it justice.

It often appears that Africa becomes especially alive at night-time and its vibrancy would be difficult to replicate in the West.

In June 1987, I travelled to Malawi and Burundi for the first time. The link with Malawi came about in such a miraculous way that I will share the story in a separate and later chapter. The link with Burundi came about through meeting David Ndaruhutse from African Revival Ministries in the Roffey Bible School near Horsham earlier that year. He had heard about our work and telephoned me while he was studying in this Bible school and, as we lived nearby, I was able to visit him and to discuss sending tea-chest consignments to his mission organisation. (African Revival Ministries later became a church called Eglise Vivante.)

During my first visit to Burundi, I was able to spend time with the Anglican Archbishop and the head of Scripture Union in Bujumbura, discussing ways of bringing clothing into the country. David felt that as these two men were held in high esteem by the government, we should have no problems if we shipped the goods in through them. A few years later, I also met David Niyozima, leader of the Eglise Evangelique des Amis based in Gitega. David had been a former student in a Bible school where David Ndaruhutse had been a teacher. In the autumn of 1990, we felt that we should start to send 20-foot container consignments to these three destinations in Burundi.

At the time of my visit, most of the missionaries had been expelled from the country and the church was only allowed to meet on Saturday afternoons and Sundays. This was not done to eliminate Christianity but to curb the power of the church. However, exciting things were happening, and David reckoned that he had seen 1,000 people converted during the three months that he had been back in the country.

In contrast with Tanzania which used to be a German and later a British colony where English was spoken by a small percentage of the population, Burundi was a French colony and French is spoken there. (Both David Ndaruhutse and David Niyonzima spoke fluently in Kirundi, French and English.) Burundi and its near neighbour, Rwanda, are also different from other East African countries because they are more mountainous in contrast to the vast plains of Tanzania. Their different terrain results in better and more regular rainfall than found in many African countries who have faced regular hardship and suffering because of poor rains.

Many of you will know that there has been conflict between the Hutu and Tutsi tribes in Burundi and Rwanda for many years. In Burundi, this conflict has flared up and then calmed down, only to flare up again and again. I will never forget David Niyonzima's testimony about an event which he witnessed during one of these periods of intense conflict. David, as leader of the Eglise Evangelique des Amis, was also responsible for their Bible school in Gitega. Most of their students were Hutu but they also had two Tutsi students. David told us how two visiting Tutsis approached them asking if they could find refuge in the Bible school and so they took them in.

After a short time, these two Tutsi visitors left the school and reported to other Tutsi colleagues that there were many Hutu students at this location. As a result, a group of Tutsis approached the Bible school unexpectedly one day with the goal of killing as many Hutus there as possible. David described how, as this Tutsi group approached the school with guns, everyone ran in different directions to hide. David hid in a work-pit under a vehicle which was parked in a garage and stayed there for about twenty hours listening to the continual gunfire and waiting until everything was quiet so that he could leave his hiding place.

Upon leaving the garage, he walked round the Bible school only to find that all the Hutu students had been killed and only the two Tutsi students remained alive. He witnessed this gruesome scene not knowing whether his wife, Felicity, and their children were alive or not. He later found them hiding with Felicity's parents. David went on to share how God challenged him and eventually enabled him to forgive the two Tutsi visitors who they had befriended, only for them to betray them.

In 1987 we also met a Ugandan pastor, Reverend Danny Kajumba, who had lived in England for sixteen years but who had been asked to return to Uganda to be part of the new government there. He had a brother, still living in Uganda, who had started a Christian organisation called "Fishers of Men". As you may remember, Uganda had suffered from many years of turmoil and violence and the economy was in a very poor condition, producing much poverty and suffering. Because of Danny Kajumba's time in the UK, there were many churches who wanted to support him when he returned to Uganda and so we thought that there would be sufficient support to start packing container consignments for Uganda. We started by packing tea-chests and later, in 1990, we started to pack container consignments for this country.

During April 1988, I travelled to Easton, Pennsylvania, USA with our daughter. I had been invited by a Presbyterian church there to help them to start packing container consignments for Uganda. As I have already written in an earlier chapter, they had heard about us through Michael Kajumba Walugembe, a Ugandan, who we had met briefly as he passed through London. We spent ten days there, visiting several different churches, sharing about our vision, and teaching them how we prepare and pack consignments.

When I visited Uganda two years later, we were very encouraged to see the tremendous work that Faith in Action (USA) had done, and spent two days visiting some of their projects, which included the sponsorship of 400 orphans. A large proportion of their container consignments had been used to benefit these orphaned children, but they were also supporting several other Christian organisations in Uganda as well.

Following our meeting with Reverend Danny Kajumba in 1987, we developed links with three more churches and a Christian hospital in Uganda during the following two years. These further links were El Shaddai Ministries and the Deliverance Church, both based in Kampala, the Anglican Diocese of Mbale and Mengo Hospital in Kampala.

I met Bishop Geresom Ilukor in June 1990, while he was in England, and we started to include boxes in our container consignments for the Diocese of Soroti who were doing wonderful work caring for Sudanese refugees in north-eastern Uganda. During June 1992, we also received a request from the co-ordinator of the Youth with a Mission ministry in Soroti Hospital asking for blankets, sheets, clothing and soap for the TB ward. The situation there was especially bad as many people had contracted TB in the refugee camps and there were insufficient resources to care for this influx of patients. We were told that many patients were lying on the concrete floor with only newspapers for mattresses and blankets, and many people were dying because of the conditions. Miraculously we had just been given 200 blankets from a local hotel and were able to respond immediately to this request. We also started to support the work of Sylvia Pinkney who was ministering to orphans through the Youth with a Mission base in Jinja.

In September 1990, Philip Playfoot, a pastor from Broadbridge Heath Free Church, and I travelled to Uganda to visit our links in this country. During this trip we were able to arrange for a 40-foot container store to be purchased and sited in the grounds of Mengo Hospital, and for David Komunda, their administrator, to co-ordinate our consignments to Uganda. It was while we were visiting one of these churches that we visited the crusade and witnessed such a dramatic demonstration of the awesome power of the name of Jesus, as I described in an earlier chapter.

While we were staying in Uganda, we travelled everywhere by minibus as the churches with whom we were working did not have their own transport. I learned that they had a very effective method of travel there which is also common in most, if not all, East African countries. In Uganda they are called "taxis", in Kenya "Matatu" and in Malawi "minibuses". I well remember the taxi park in Kampala. It covered a large area of ground with hundreds of small minibuses packed into this large space with drivers and ticket collectors all shouting out loudly, advertising the destination to which they were travelling. Slowly these minibuses filled up and when they were full, they left for their advertised destination. Very often they would not stop on route and so once they had left, each destination was reached quickly, easily and cheaply. Perhaps this is a system which we would do well to learn from!

During 1986, we also started to pack tea-chests for an orphanage in Zambia through a contact that we had made in the UK, and during 1987, we met a couple who were living in Whitstable in Kent who had lived for six years in Bophuthatswana, one of the "homelands" in South Africa. Following some TV programmes showing the very poor living conditions in these homelands, we started to pack tea-chests of clothing for this region of South Africa.

Early in 1991, I met Florence Phiri while visiting Agnes Mkoko, a leader of the Mothers' Union in Malawi, while she was attending an Anglican conference in the Midlands. Florence was the leader of the Mothers' Union in

Zambia and was attending the same conference. Following this meeting, I spent a week visiting Zambia in August 1991 and spent a very enjoyable and informative week visiting the bishop and many Mothers' Union events in that country. After this visit, we started to pack container consignments for the Anglican Church in this country and these consignments were to be co-ordinated by Florence.

At the beginning of 1995, David Ndaruhutse, together with some members of his church, moved from Burundi to Rwanda so that they could start a church there. During that same year, we were contacted by a member of the Anglican church in Maidenhead, a church where they had strong links with the Anglican church in Rwanda through family members who had been missionaries in that country for many years. We therefore started to pack container consignments for Rwanda, and these were co-ordinated by this church in Maidenhead. We sent our first container to Rwanda during October of that same year.

As in Burundi, the conflict in Rwanda is also between the Hutu and Tutsi tribes. In both countries the Hutu are the majority with about 85 per cent of the population. In Rwanda, the Hutus had been in power for many years and during the 1960s, thousands of Tutsis left Rwanda and fled mainly to Uganda. An especially brutal conflict between these two tribes started in 1990 and built up to 100 days of very violent slaughter between 7th April and 15th July 1994. During this conflict the Tutsi gained control of the country and about one million of the Tutsi refugees returned. As about one million were killed in the conflict the population remained the same. By 1995, the situation had become stable and church buildings were being reconstructed, leaders were being trained and many were turning to Christ for forgiveness. If they had killed others, they felt that only Christ could forgive them and thus many were running into the church for refuge and peace.

Following David's move to Rwanda, he started to set up churches, orphanages and clinics there. He told us that when he first went into the camps the people did not respond positively to their gospel message, but as he started to give out our clothing, so their hearts were softened by this demonstration of love, and afterwards thousands crowded around to listen to the message of God's wonderful love for them.

On Saturday 13th September 1997, we received the tragic news that David Ndaruhutse had died in an airplane crash the previous day. We understand that he was travelling from Rwanda to Zaire to participate in a crusade with fifteen pastors and five evangelists when their plane hit a mountain and burst into flames. All the passengers were killed, the bodies beyond recognition. We learned later that 32,000 people attended the funeral.

We had known and worked with David for ten years and throughout this time he had worked tirelessly in the Lord's service in Burundi, Rwanda, Tanzania, Uganda and Zaire. Through his faithful ministry many thousands of people met with God and found their salvation. Just before his death, David had been working in north-eastern Zaire, where they had seen many thousands receive salvation. We understand that David had told a friend that this work in Zaire was the fulfilment of his life-long hopes and dreams and he felt sure that this was the beginning of revival. He added that he was now ready to depart this life should the Lord wish to call him home.

We also understand that before he died, David had visited Edmund Kivuye, his nephew and leader of the church in Burundi, and had given him the jacket which he always wore, telling him that the Lord had told him to hand his "mantle" over to him. Through these events, David must have sensed something of his imminent death, although he had not told anyone.

I felt very challenged by this tragic, but glorious incident. I asked myself two questions: first, when I die, will I have fulfilled all the work that the Lord has prepared for me to do? Second, am I sufficiently humble and sensitive to the voice of the Holy Spirit, to be able to lay down my ministry as David did?

By the beginning of 1996, we were packing container consignments for eight different locations in six countries in East Africa and tea-chests for Bophuthatswana in South Africa, having set up ninety-two packing groups in the UK and having received all the finances necessary to ship the sixty-seven container consignments that we had sent up until this time. All these links were miraculously opened up for us by God and are a wonderful demonstration of His faithfulness. When He makes a promise, He is faithful to keep that promise when we trust in Him and do not try to achieve things without His miraculous help.

These early years were both exciting and challenging. I met many amazing people and was able to learn a great deal about African culture from the many friendships that I made with local people. My ability to get cheap stand-by tickets meant that most of my travelling was done alone as other people would have to pay the full price and we would face difficulties if I was not able to get on our planned flights. This was often difficult but resulted in many important benefits. First, I had no one to trust but God and so I learnt to depend increasingly on Him. Second, I developed much better relationships with the many amazing Africans whom I met because I was not distracted by the ease of talking with English-speaking travelling companions.

The most significant lesson that I learnt was to trust in the awesome faithfulness of God as He led me from place to place, showed me how He wanted me to work and looked after my every need. I faced many difficulties but, in every situation, He enabled me to overcome. He also rescued me and healed me on many different occasions.

There were many occasions when I was sick. I had malaria twice even though I was taking prophylactics because, during the early years, I had a casual approach to using a mosquito net. Fortunately, on both occasions the malaria did not develop until after I arrived home and I was therefore able to get treatment in the comfort of my own home. I soon learnt that using a mosquito net is important! This experience gave me a small glimpse of the enormous suffering that is caused by this very common and dreadful disease. I was to learn later that cerebral malaria can quickly and easily kill its victim, especially when they are children. We were later to start a project to protect people from this common killer.

Being unused to African food, I also used to suffer regularly from diarrhoea and sickness during the early years. Foolishly, I used to travel light without medicines to deal with these minor emergencies. I well remember several occasions when I was due to travel out to a village during the day and knew that I could not cancel the visit because a church meeting and meal would have been prepared for our visit. In faith, I left the European house with a toilet where I was staying knowing that I was ill, but as soon as I left the house the diarrhoea stopped until I returned home that evening.

There was one occasion when I was staying with the Tanzanian pastor of a church in Dar es Salaam and was due to speak at a ladies' meeting in the church below his flat that afternoon. Suffering from both diarrhoea and sickness, I prayed desperately for God to heal me. He told me that He would heal me when I got to the meeting and so I had to walk out of the flat in faith – only to find that immediately I walked out of the door the diarrhoea and sickness left. I learned through these experiences that, like Peter, we need to take a risky step of faith out of a place of perceived safety before we see the miraculous.

In Uganda, I could have been seriously hurt when my shoulder bag was cut with a knife. The knife could have cut my arm as well, but it did not. Neither did I lose any items in the bag – the aim of this attack – as the cut only extended along the width but not the two sides of the bag. I did not even know, at the time, what had happened. It was my colleagues who noticed the cut a short time later. In Burundi, my shoulder bag was nearly stolen. I was sitting in the centre of one of the back seats of a small minibus when an arm came suddenly through the window with the aim of grabbing it. Fortunately, I grabbed hold of the bag just in time.

I have tried, in this chapter, to record briefly the key events of these early years of travelling. What I did not realise at the time was that the adventure had barely begun!

Chapter 11

Giving and Receiving

Genesis 22:9-14: "⁹ When they reached the place God had told him about, Abraham built an altar there and arranged the wood on it. He bound his son Isaac and laid him on the altar, on top of the wood. ¹⁰ Then he reached out his hand and took the knife to slay his son. ¹¹ But the angel of the LORD called out to him from heaven, 'Abraham! Abraham!' 'Here I am,' he replied. ¹² 'Do not lay a hand on the boy,' he said. 'Do not do anything to him. Now I know that you fear God, because you have not withheld from me your son, your only son.' ¹³ Abraham looked up and there in a thicket he saw a ram caught by its horns. He went over and took the ram and sacrificed it as a burnt offering instead of his son. ¹⁴ So Abraham called that place The LORD Will Provide. And to this day it is said, 'On the mountain of the LORD it will be provided.'"

While God was demonstrating His wonderful faithfulness to multiply the work which we had started, He was also teaching us to trust Him to provide for us as well. You will remember my sharing in an earlier chapter how God had challenged us to trust Him to provide all the finances that we need, asking us not to fund-raise or to ask for financial provision. Throughout the following years and right up to the present time, we have continued to learn important lessons about trusting God with all our financial needs, and this not only applies to our ministry in Africa but also in our personal lives as well.

Shortly after we had started to pack as a group, we started the legal process of registering our charity with the Charity Commission in the UK. This was not completed until June 1986. The Trust Deed upon which the charity is based gives our projected annual income as £10,000 which we considered to be an enormous step of faith at that time. Some thirty plus years later, we continue to obey the Lord's command not to solicit for funds in any way and we regularly receive between £50,000 and £110,000 each year, having received a total of over £2.5 million over the last thirty-three years.

We should remember that all these figures quoted at the beginning of this chapter were worth considerably more in 1986 than they would be today.

During this time, we have never fund-raised in any way or asked for any funds for anything. I am convinced that if we had tried to raise this money through our own efforts, we would never have been able to raise anything like this amount. Furthermore, we have not needed to spend time or finances trying to raise the necessary financial support for our work. A further very significant advantage is that the continual multiplication of our work and the provision of all the finances which we need is a constant encouragement that God is with us and that this ministry is His plan for our lives and not just our "good idea"! It also, I believe, glorifies the Lord and is a testimony to other people when we share about His wonderful faithfulness to us. When we depend on Him for continual support, multiplication and provision, this also helps to keep us focused on His plans and not our own.

Initially, Martin and I trusted God for the finances to send all the boxes that other groups had packed, and I can testify honestly that we never had a bill that we could not pay. We did once receive a bill for the transportation of a container to Tanzania and a cheque that covered the extra funds needed to pay it in the same post. We do now ask our packing groups to pay for the transport of their boxes. However, this only accounts for about 10-15 per cent of our annual income and many packing groups have testified of the miraculous provision of finances that they have seen which has enabled them to pay for their boxes. One reason that prompted us to ask packing groups to pay for the transportation of their own boxes was a desire to maintain the high standard of all the boxes included in our consignments and we felt that this would be a very practical way to achieve this goal.

Upon Martin's return from his second visit to Tanzania, our first container consignment was full and ready to leave. During the first year of this new ministry, about four tons of goods went through our house and as the work grew our house became too small for both an office and storage space for packing materials!

Miraculously, in the October of that second year, we were offered £50,000 to purchase a house where we would have more space. This was before we had even contemplated our need to move. We soon found a beautiful cottage with a large garden. We moved into our new cottage in April of the following year (1986), at no cost whatsoever to ourselves.

As the actual building was no larger than our previous house, we needed to put up buildings in the garden for packing and storage. Once again God was to provide miraculously for these: about three years previously, Martin had been given some shares in his airline. However, these shares had no value for us as no dividend was paid and – because it was a private company – Martin could not sell them to anyone. This very month, however, his company went public and this worthless piece of paper became worth £60,000 overnight! How can we ever doubt the faithfulness of God?

We discovered that the maximum number of shares that we could sell each year without paying capital gains tax would be £6,000 and so we sold this amount to purchase the buildings that we needed. When we drove up to Derbyshire to look at the wooden chalet-type buildings that we wanted to purchase for the garden, we were told that they were in the process of dismantling their show-site. At first, we thought our trip had been in vain but we soon realised what a blessing in disguise this was as we were able to buy one large and two smaller models from this show-site for £2,700, instead of buying one large building for about £9,000 as we had planned. Then, having paid for these three buildings, we received an unexpected cheque for £3,000 with the instructions: "This is to pay for your new buildings!"

The financial gifts for our new house and storage buildings together with the new value of Martin's shares made a total of about £113,000 which had been provided in one six-week period during this year. We were later given a gift of £21,000 from a business friend of my father who stipulated that we should use it to maintain a cash flow. We also saw that the yearly amount of £6,000, which we could raise each year from the sale of Martin's shares, would be a wonderful increased provision for the work. We later used some of this money to extend our house to include an office. Several years later, Martin's airline ceased trading and his share certificate became worthless once again. This was an important lesson about the lack of security that finances will provide for it is impossible to keep them safe and they can be lost, stolen or destroyed at any time and without any notice.

As we have continued to obey God's instructions never to ask for money, we have discovered in a deeper and deeper way the tremendous blessings of depending on Him on a daily basis. We have not only seen miracles of provision in the UK, but we have also witnessed the abundant and miraculous generosity of God in Africa as well. I will describe some of these in a later chapter.

In considering this important subject of God as our Provider, I have learnt many lessons from the gospel story of the Feeding of the Five Thousand. In the early years, the Lord used it to show me both my role and His role in the work of our ministry: I was to give what I had, and He would multiply the work. More recently, He has showed me further important truths from this well-known story.

> John 6:5-13: "[5] When Jesus looked up and saw a great crowd coming towards him, he said to Philip, 'Where shall we buy bread for these people to eat?' [6] He asked this only to test him, for he already had in mind what he was going to do. [7] Philip answered him, 'It would take more than half a year's wages to buy enough bread for each one to have a bite!' [8] Another of his disciples, Andrew, Simon Peter's brother, spoke up, [9] 'Here is a boy with five small barley loaves and two small fish, but how far will they go among so many?' [10] Jesus said, 'Make the people sit down.' There was plenty of grass in that place, and they sat down (about five thousand men were there). [11] Jesus then took the loaves, gave thanks, and distributed to those who were seated as much as they wanted. He did the same with the fish. [12] When they had all had enough to eat, he said to his disciples, 'Gather the pieces that are left over. Let nothing be wasted.' [13] So they gathered them and filled twelve baskets with the pieces of the five barley loaves left over by those who had eaten."

The above quoted passage is taken from the gospel of John, but we also find this same story in the gospels of Matthew, Mark and Luke. As we read through this story, I would like us to consider the difference between the attitude, words and behaviour of the disciples and those of Jesus. This story is especially relevant to situations where we do not have enough to meet the needs which we face.

In verse eight, Andrew's response to the donation of the five loaves and two fish is that they were not enough for this large crowd. (This fact is true if you look at the event simply from a worldly point of view.) However, from a spiritual perspective we need to ask ourselves how often we have the same attitude as these disciples. We look at what we have, and we do not think that it is enough. We focus on what we do not have, and not on what we have. We are not satisfied with or grateful for what God has provided for us and we often look to others to provide for us. We see ourselves as beneficiaries and not donors. If this is our attitude, I believe that we will continue to live a life of insufficiency.

We also do the same with our character and abilities as well as with our finances and possessions – we consider ourselves lacking in some way. We undermine ourselves, seeing ourselves as too young or too old, too poor, too weak or in poor health, or lacking sufficient education or training; forgetting that God chooses the weak, the foolish and the insignificant to shame the strong, the wise and those who are important in the eyes of the world. We think that we have too little to give and we need to remind ourselves that if the little boy had not given his food, which was too little, no one would have been fed.

> 1 Corinthians 1:26-31: "[26] Brothers and sisters, think of what you were when you were called. Not many of you were wise by human standards; not many were influential; not many were of noble birth. [27] But God chose the foolish things of the world to shame the wise; God chose the weak things of the world to shame the strong. [28] God chose the lowly things of this world and the despised things – and the things that are not – to nullify the things that are, [29] so that no one may boast before him. [30] It is because of him that you are in Christ Jesus, who has become for us wisdom from God – that is, our righteousness, holiness and redemption. [31] Therefore, as it is written: 'Let the one who boasts boast in the Lord.'"

Jesus' attitude was completely different. First, He gave thanks for what they had – even though it was far too little for the vast crowd. Second, He told the people to sit down and asked the disciples to distribute this small amount of food to everyone. When they did this, there was plenty for everyone and even some left over. This, I believe, is the lesson which we need to learn and to apply: we should first be grateful for what we have, even if it is not enough for our needs, then thank God for it and share what little we have with others.

Let us remember that if we want to see the miraculous, we need to follow Paul's example and walk by faith and not by sight. We need to learn not to look at our circumstances from a worldly point of view but consider the transformation that Jesus has won for us on the cross and the many promises given to us in God's Word. We may be weak, uneducated, poor, fearful and lacking in self-confidence but any work that we do for God is not dependent on our ability and resources but on His. When we change the way that we perceive ourselves, our life will change for the better as well.

2 Corinthians 5:7: "For we live by faith, not by sight."

I will share more about some of the miraculous provision that we have seen in a later chapter together with some lessons about having the right attitude towards money and the challenging principle of "sowing and reaping".

Chapter 12

Malawi, the Warm Heart of Africa

Jeremiah 29:11: "'For I know the plans I have for you,' declares the LORD, 'plans to prosper you and not to harm you, plans to give you hope and a future.'"

As I have already mentioned in an earlier chapter, I visited Tanzania, Burundi and Malawi during June 1987. I travelled alone and had ten different flights, all on a "space-available" basis, and there was a seat for me on every flight. Following this trip, we started to pack 20-foot container consignments for the El Shaddai independent church in Malawi and smaller consignments for Scripture Union in Burundi.

The link with this church in Malawi came about in a truly miraculous way and was to lead to an amazing relationship with the church and a significant increase in our ministry. The previous summer, two friends in our church had visited a church in America where they were holding a Christian camp for young people. A short time after their return to the UK, they received a newsletter which had been written by a lady who was a friend of their American hosts. This friend had written a newsletter while visiting Malawi and working briefly with Pastor Lameck Msamange who had a wonderful ministry in the Mozambican refugee camps in southern Malawi. (There was a civil war in Mozambique at that time and about a million refugees had crossed the border into Malawi.)

Knowing about the work that we had started, our church friends passed this letter to us. The newsletter spoke about the wonderful work that Lameck was doing and of the tremendous need in these refugee camps. As I read this letter, God spoke one single word very clearly: "Go." (I should add that we have received a great number of letters all asking us to provide both finances and resources for churches in many different countries, but I have only heard clear direction from God on this one occasion.) I was not even sure exactly where Malawi was and had to check its exact location in an atlas. (I would, of course, search on Google now!)

My first response was to write to this American lady thinking that she was still in Malawi, but she had already returned to America and I did not therefore receive any reply. Fortunately, as it turned out, I persevered and wrote a letter to Pastor Msamange, whose address was also in this newsletter, at the beginning of the following year. Lameck replied promptly to my letter and we arranged a visit during June that year, a visit which was to develop into an amazing friendship with the church leaders of this independent church but started with my offer to pack consignments of clothing for them to distribute.

I learned later that Lameck had also been travelling into Mozambique and had been very concerned about their need for clothing. Some ladies only had fertiliser sacks to wear and these were wrapped around them in the same way that they wear their khangas. About one month before he received my letter, he had prayed about this need for clothing and had felt that God was asking him to share some of his own clothing with them. However, he and his family had very little and so he initially struggled with this request. After praying for several days and receiving the same answer, he reluctantly asked his family to divide their clothing into half and he took this into Mozambique for distribution. About one month later, he received my letter.

Over the last thirty-one years we have sent thirty-two 20-foot container consignments to Malawi and some smaller consignments as well. This would amount to about 20,000 garments and is a wonderful example of a principle which we considered in an earlier chapter when we considered the story of the Feeding of the Five Thousand: when we are prepared to share what we have, even when it is very little, God will multiply it to provide for a multitude. It is also a fulfilment of Jesus' promise in the gospel of Luke. I also believe that in sharing his family's small amount of clothing, Lameck had demonstrated that he could be trusted to share a much larger amount.

Luke 6:38: "Give, and it will be given to you. A good measure, pressed down, shaken together and running over, will be poured into your lap. For with the measure you use, it will be measured to you."

My first visit to Malawi did not appear to start well. As I was travelling on stand-by tickets, I was not able to be precise about the flight on which I would be arriving. There were in fact two flights from Lilongwe, the capital of Malawi, to Blantyre where the church was based. Unfortunately, Lameck had misunderstood my letter and went to collect me from the second flight when I was able to get on the first.

This meant that when I arrived alone in Chileka Airport, in a country that I had never visited before and where I did not know anyone, there was no one to meet me! Fortunately, I had got into conversation with some other passengers from that flight and they very kindly offered to take me to a local Christian guest house called the Grace Bandawe Guest House. I well remember booking into a room and sitting on my bed wondering what I should do. The only address which I had for Lameck was a post office box number and his telephone was not working. I therefore had no means of contacting him. Amazingly, I felt peaceful.

The very kind lady who ran this guest house said that she knew Lameck and that he always drove his children to school each morning along the road outside this guest house. She suggested that we stood by the roadside early the following morning so that she could recognise him and stop his car. Fortunately, as it turned out, this was not necessary as later that afternoon, Lameck and another pastor, Samuel Soko, came looking for me. They had gone to collect me from the later flight and upon finding that I was not on that flight, realised that this was the most likely place that I would be.

This first visit to Malawi only lasted for three to four days but it was to have a profound impact on our future ministry. In all the other African countries that I had visited, I was always welcomed most warmly and offered very generous hospitality. On no occasion could I find any fault in the way that I was looked after. However, there was a profound difference in one respect between my visit to this church in Malawi and all the other churches in other countries that I have visited over many years: in all the other churches I was taken to different locations and projects so that I could see the work that they were doing. In Malawi, Lameck invited me to be part of what they were doing. Instead of simply being a spectator, I was invited to work with them as a member of their church leadership team and this was to make a profound difference in our relationship with this church.

From this very first visit, I was convinced that the link was to be very significant for us. Upon my return to the UK, I prayed for guidance and felt that the Lord spoke to me from the gospel of Luke, chapter 5. In this passage, Luke tells how Jesus borrowed Peter's boat to enable Him to speak to the crowd which were following Him. You may remember this story: after Jesus had finished speaking, He asked Peter to go out into the deep and to lower his nets. Peter replied that they had fished all night and caught nothing but because of Jesus' word he would lower the nets again. When they did this, they caught such a large number of fish that their nets were almost breaking. They therefore signalled to their partners to come and to help them and they filled up both boats so that they began to sink. I felt that the Lord was saying through this story that there would be such a large growth in this church that they needed us in the UK to help them to care for the large crowd that would come to salvation through their ministry.

During November of that same year, I visited Dodoma and Dar es Salaam in Tanzania and returned to southern Malawi for a few days. While I was in Malawi, God spoke very clearly to me about giving regular financial support to this church as well as sending consignments of clothing. This very clear guidance came about in this way: one Saturday afternoon during this trip, Lameck shared with me about some difficulties they were facing with the link that he had made with the lady from America, the same person whose newsletter I had been given.

He did not go into a lot of details, he simply shared that he did not think that his vision was compatible with hers. He was, however, in a difficult position because they were now dependent on the finances that they were receiving from this link in America. I replied that I believed God was asking him to decide about whether to continue with this relationship, which was troubling him, before God would provide any alternative provision.

The following day, a Sunday, we had planned to visit some churches in the afternoon. As I was staying in the Grace Bandawe Guest House, I decided to walk across the road and to attend the church opposite. I believe that it was a Presbyterian church, but I cannot be sure.

The sermon was all about the work of the Holy Spirit and although – thirty-one years later – I cannot remember much about it, I do very clearly remember the minister speaking about the way in which the Holy Spirit comes alongside us to guide us and to teach us what He wants us to do. He went on to say that we need to be sensitive and responsive to His prompting so that we do not miss the opportunities presented to us. He then gave various examples of this including words to this effect: "It may be that a friend of yours is facing various difficulties and God is asking you to help him, and if you do not offer to help him now, you may lose the opportunity that God is offering you." Together with these words came the absolute assurance that God was asking us to give regular financial support to this church.

I did not share this with Lameck during this trip as I needed to discuss this new direction with Martin first. At that time, we had almost no money in our Faith in Action bank account in the UK, but miraculously Martin agreed to take this step of faith and after we had agreed to give financial support to this church and had arranged to transfer £350 each month to Malawi, a greatly increased flow of money started to pour in for our work and we always had sufficient to send the promised amount each month. Added to this, within six years our average payment to this church would increase from £350 to between £3,000 and £5,000 each month. By the time that I returned to Malawi the following year, Lameck had already cut his links with America.

Most of Malawi is high plateau but the very southern tip drops right down to sea level. It is approached by a steep escarpment which descends about 1,000 metres to these plains below. This area is named the Lower Shire from the River Shire which flows down the centre towards Mozambique and the Indian Ocean. It was in this area that Lameck had started to preach two years earlier. (I will share his testimony and how he came to be evangelising in southern Malawi in the following chapter.)

When I first visited Malawi in 1987, Lameck had set up about fifty churches in this southern area of the country in which most of the villages had never heard the gospel and where the whole region was steeped in witchcraft. So much so, Lameck told me that he used to sleep in his car at the very beginning because of the very dark spiritual atmosphere in most of the houses. Some thirty-one years later they now have about 1,000 churches in Malawi, Mozambique, Zimbabwe and Zambia.

The Lower Shire is very much the forgotten region of the country and is triangular, tapering down to a point in the very south. In all my travels – possibly fifty plus visits to this region – I only remember seeing one European person on one occasion. It is not only the forgotten and ignored region of the country, but it is also the poorest and most in need of support. The Sena tribe who live there are even looked down on by the other tribes in the country. It is most in need because being lower than the rest of the country and surrounded on two and a half sides of the triangle by high hills, it suffers from all weather extremes. When the rains are poor, it is hotter and drier than the rest of the country. When the rains are heavy, surface water runs down the escarpment and fills up the region rather like a basin. Even after thirty-one years, most of the churches in this group of churches are based in this area.

During one of my visits to Malawi in 1988, Lameck asked whether they could register their church with the name Faith in Action. We agreed to his request and this registration in Malawi was completed quickly. This church is separate from our charity in the UK, and neither of us have any legal authority over the other. Later in 1988, Lameck and his colleague, Peter Guta, made their first of several trips to the UK so that they could visit, encourage and inspire our packing groups who were packing for Malawi. This trip, as all later trips, was extremely successful.

These early visits to Malawi marked the beginning of a significant change to the ministry of Faith in Action in the UK. The work of packing container consignments of relief aid continued although some years later we asked the churches who were co-ordinating our consignments for other countries if they would take full responsibility for this aspect of our work, leaving us to focus on Malawi. (This step became necessary because all our administrative work is done on a voluntary basis and we were finding it increasingly difficult to administer this significant increase in our ministry. This change would also give these other churches the freedom to develop their African link in a way that was appropriate for them.) Beginning in 1988, we began working in a variety of different ways to support the Faith in Action Church in Malawi. The scope of our ministry in this country continues to grow and I will go on to describe this growth together with some of the adventures and miracles that we have seen in later chapters.

Chapter 13

Pastor Lameck Msamange

John 15:16: "You did not choose me, but I chose you and appointed you so that you might go and bear fruit – fruit that will last – and so that whatever you ask in my name the Father will give you."

With his permission, I will share Lameck's very challenging testimony as he has shared it in various meetings where I have been present. It is another story which shows the amazing way in which God transforms our lives regardless of the difficulties and pain of our early years. It also shows Lameck's whole-hearted commitment to serve God, even to the point of risking his own life for the sake of the gospel. It is a story which should challenge and encourage us all in our own personal journey of faith.

Lameck was born on 24th August 1957 in Malemia Village in the very south of Malawi. His uncle was a village chief and Lameck inherited this position much later after his uncle had died. This was to give him the opportunity to work with the government in Malawi as well as leading the Faith in Action Church. When he was two years old, his parents divorced and his mother was left to look after the children with no income. Lameck tells me that six of his older siblings died from malnutrition. His mother therefore attempted to provide for her family by brewing beer for sale. However, as this was illegal in Malawi at the time, she was put into prison for two years from 1959 to 1961 and Lameck had to go with her. This memory is still a painful one for him. Shortly after she was released, she took Lameck and his remaining siblings to Zimbabwe.

Following their arrival in Zimbabwe and because of the death of his siblings, Lameck's father – who had also moved to Zimbabwe with his new wife – took him away from his mother so that he could live with him. Although this move probably saved his life, his father was an alcoholic and in his drunken moments would beat Lameck on a regular basis. His childhood was therefore both poor and unhappy and he tells me that he got his first pair of shoes out of a dustbin when he was thirteen years old. Despite his unhappy relationship with his father, Lameck was able to lead both his parents to Christ before they died.

As he grew up, Lameck became more and more resentful and much of this resentment was aimed towards the British who ruled Zimbabwe at that time. As you may know, both the British leaders in Zimbabwe and the Portuguese leaders in Mozambique were able to resist the move to independence during the 1960s when most East African countries found their freedom. Zimbabwe did not become independent until 18th April 1980.

In 1964, aged just seven, Lameck joined a socialist inspired political group called the Black Shadows. Several years later, their leader was wanted by the police and there were posters showing his picture asking for people to report him if they were aware of his location. This group hated the British and especially Christians as they linked the two together. They used to say that missionaries had come to their country and after telling them to shut their eyes to pray, had stolen their country! Also, Lameck had worked as a "garden-boy" for a British family where the wife had treated him with great disrespect. We have often joked since about God's sense of humour in sending another "White British Lady" to work with him.

Lameck was living in a township on the edge of Harare, the capital of Zimbabwe. One day they saw posters pinned up in their township advertising a Christian crusade. As a group, they decided that they would attend this crusade with the sole aim of disrupting and destroying the meeting. They prepared themselves by filling their pockets with sticks, stones and broken bottles and agreed that they would wait for their leader to give the sign for them to begin to cause mayhem.

Lameck tells me that they all went to the meeting on 4th April 1971 and sat together. After the singing, the preacher stood up and spoke from the gospel of Matthew, chapter 11, verse 28. Lameck comments with humour how relevant this passage was as they were all heavy-laden with sticks, stones and broken bottles!

Matthew 11:28: "Come to Me, all who are weary and heavy-laden, and I will give you rest." (NASB)

Meanwhile, they all waited for a sign from their leader, but it did not come as he was transfixed by the message and when it finished and an altar call was given, he was the first to go up to the front and told all the other members of the group, including Lameck, to follow him! When they went to the front, each one of them was prayed for individually and Lameck describes how, as he was being prayed for, all the hatred just melted away and he felt a wonderful anointing of love. He also tells me that this whole group have remained faithful to this commitment to a new and radically different life.

The following day their leader, who was wanted by the police, went into the police station to give himself up. Apparently, he pointed to his poster hanging on the wall and told them that he was that man and that he had come to give himself up as last night Jesus had arrested him! Amazingly, the policeman on duty replied that as Jesus had forgiven him, then they would also forgive him, and he was free to go!

Following his wonderful conversion, Lameck's life changed radically. He forgave his parents and renewed his relationship with them. He also started to give out tracts telling others about salvation. On 3rd April 1976, Lameck married Rebecca and started to travel into southern Malawi (his birthplace) to preach the gospel as well as continuing to preach in Zimbabwe.

Several years later, he got hold of the book *God's Smuggler* by Brother Andrew, a young Dutch missionary who started his international ministry by smuggling Bibles into communist Russia. Lameck read it hungrily and was so impressed with Brother Andrew's testimony that he wrote to their base in Holland saying how much he had enjoyed this book. He was very surprised when he received a reply from Brother Andrew himself, saying that they were considering setting up a new base in Zimbabwe – smuggling Bibles into communist Mozambique – and asking whether he would be interested in heading up this new branch. Lameck replied in the affirmative.

Mozambique had gained independence in 1975 and the Portuguese were replaced by Frelimo, the new communist government. However, a civil war between the Portuguese and adherents of the old regime (Renamo) and the Frelimo government continued for many years. Almost immediately the communist government started to persecute the church. Many thousands of Christians were martyred and almost all their Bibles were burned.

As Lameck tells his story, he quickly proceeds to share about their first trip into Mozambique. Just prior to this first trip, he had heard from a friend who had been caught smuggling gospel tracts in that same country and who had been imprisoned for six months for carrying just two gospel tracts. As they had filled their vehicle with Bibles, they realised how much greater the punishment would be if they were caught with this large forbidden load. Also, with Lameck's experience of prison when he was a child, this would have been an especially difficult risk for him to take.

Lameck and two colleagues made this first trip. As they left Harare, they were filled with excitement and were singing praise songs to build their spirits. However, as they came closer and closer to the border, they became quieter and quieter, becoming increasingly concerned about the danger ahead. When they came to the border, they had no difficulty processing their exit documents at the Zimbabwe border post. However, the entrance into Mozambique would not prove to be so easy. Lameck told his colleagues that he would go and get their documents processed and he asked them to pray.

He had no difficulties getting their passports stamped for entry into Mozambique but when Lameck went to the customs desk, the official asked him whether he had anything to declare! Lameck realised that, as a Christian, it would not be acceptable for him to lie and so he replied: "Some things." There followed a rather brief conversation between him and the customs official. The conversation went something like this: "What things." "Some things." "What things." "Some things." "What things!"

Eventually, Lameck decided to tell the truth. He said, "I have a car full of Bibles!" The customs officer thought that he was teasing him for surely, he must have thought, no one would own up to carrying Bibles into a Marxist country. He became very angry and, thumping his fist on his desk, said, "Young man, do not mess about with me. Get into your car right now and drive across the border!"

The jubilation in the car after this amazing miracle must have been a wonderful relief. However, they were now presented with a further very significant problem. This was their first visit into Mozambique, and they did not have any contacts there. It would have been very dangerous for them to go up to anyone and to ask if they were a Christian. They therefore kept driving, wondering what they could do. Eventually they arrived at the coast and, having run low in fuel, drove into a garage in Beira.

As Lameck was filling the car with fuel, he noticed a group of young men sitting on the curb, at the edge of the garage. One of these young men approached him and whispered in his ear, "You have Bibles for us!" Lameck was immediately wary. Was this a trick set up by a communist official to catch anyone with Bibles? "Please do not worry," said his new-found friend. "We are a group of Christians who live on the edge of Beira. We were attending a prayer meeting this Tuesday and God spoke to us and said that someone driving a vehicle with a foreign registration plate would bring us Bibles and that we should come to this garage and wait for him!" How can we ever doubt the wonderful goodness and faithfulness of God when we step out in faith in obedience to Him!

In 1983, after working with Open Doors in Zimbabwe for several years, they asked Lameck if he would be prepared to go to Malawi and to start working in the Mozambican refugee camps in the south of that country. He also continued to travel into Mozambique. It was Open Doors who later sent Lameck to America to speak about their work in Mozambique, and this is where he met the lady who had written the newsletter mentioned in the previous chapter. In 1986, Lameck resigned from Open Doors shortly before they withdrew from their work in Malawi.

Lameck is a natural evangelist who has led many thousands to Christ during his life. He had already been evangelising in Zimbabwe and so it was only natural for him to start sharing his faith in Malawi. However, in Zimbabwe there had been churches for these new converts to join, whereas the area in Malawi where he started to share his faith was very different. Quite naturally he started to preach in the Lower Shire, the area in the very south of Malawi which I mentioned in the previous chapter. There were two reasons for this: first, most of the Mozambican refugee camps were based in this area and second, this is the area where he was born. As there were very few churches in the area and many villages had never heard the gospel, Lameck had little choice but to start a church in this area. When I arrived just four years after Lameck had returned to Malawi, they had already started about fifty churches.

When I first arrived in Malawi in 1987, Lameck and his wife, Rebecca, had five children: Andrew, Lawrence, Wesley, Arnold and Patience. They later had two more boys: Lameck Junior and Beniah. Tragically, Arnold died suddenly a few years ago, we think due to complications after having TB.

In the early years, Lameck was working with three other men: Peter Guta, Harry Khembo and Rankeni Ngowera. Benson Kaisi joined them within a year or so to look after their vehicles. This church leadership team grew quickly to include Dan Nkhandwe, Mark Siteche, Julius Phiri, and more recently two of Lameck's grown-up sons: Wesley and Lawrence Msamange.

During the many years that I have been visiting Malawi, Lameck has been attacked on three different occasions. The first time was when a group of about twenty-five men broke into their house during the night and Lameck was hit over the head with a panga – a heavy tool with a metal blade which they use for cutting grass – while trying to protect his wife. He did receive good medical care immediately afterwards but has suffered from regular headaches since.

In the second attack, his attacker had set an ambush for him while he was driving towards his house. Fortunately, he was able to reverse quickly enough to escape. We think that this second attack was specifically aimed at him due to jealousy because of all the financial resources that his church receives from the West. In my experience, this type of jealousy is common in Africa. We are not sure whether the third attack was another personal attack or whether his attacker was simply trying to burgle their house and during this attack he was hit on the head once again. Lameck also suffered from quite a serious stroke a few years ago but has very miraculously made a full recovery.

Sadly, Rankeni died from yellow fever during the early years, and more recently Peter died from diabetes and Mark died following a stroke, leaving five in the leadership team based in Blantyre and Harry Khembo as one of many area pastors based in the Lower Shire. They also have a large network of area pastors and pastors who look after their 600 plus churches in Malawi. Added to this, they have churches in Mozambique, Zimbabwe and Zambia.

Chapter 14

The Blessing of Generosity

Luke 6:38: "Give, and it will be given to you. A good measure, pressed down, shaken together and running over, will be poured into your lap. For with the measure you use, it will be measured to you."

In an earlier chapter, we considered the miraculous way in which God provided vast quantities of clothing for Malawi after Lameck had given half of his own family's clothing away. This miraculous demonstration of God's provision introduces another lesson which I have learned, as quoted in the above verse from the gospel of Luke: the measure that we deal out to others will be the measure that we receive. We can therefore determine what we will receive by the amount that we first give away.

All of God's principles are extremely powerful, but most of them are also irrational to the worldly mind, and this is especially true with the lesson about giving and receiving. This is one reason why we can so easily miss God's best. A worldly mind will think: I do not have enough money to meet my own financial needs and so I need to hold on to what I have and even ask others to help me. God's Word teaches us the exact opposite: I do have enough and so I need to give a generous amount away! We find this principle taught throughout the New Testament and I have experienced many situations where God has been very faithful to this promise when we have obeyed this challenging instruction. We have already looked at one biblical example: when the small boy gave away his lunch, which was very little and not nearly enough for the vast crowd, there was more than enough for everyone.

Let us first look at biblical teaching on this important subject of money before I share further evidence that this principle is powerfully true. It applies to possessions as well as money, as we saw with Lameck's experience with clothing, but we will focus mainly on the issue of finances for simplicity. The Bible speaks a great deal about issues relating to money and this gives an indication of the importance that God places on us having a good attitude towards it.

Because there is so much unbalanced and incorrect teaching about finances and prosperity in the church, I believe that it is especially important to have a balanced biblical view of this subject of wealth and God's wonderful provision. If we want to see God provide for whatever ministry He calls us to, we need to first ensure that we have a right attitude towards wealth and prosperity. If our attitude towards money is wrong, it is very unlikely that we will see God giving us anymore. We will therefore consider six passages which teach us lessons about the danger of having a wrong attitude towards wealth before we go on to consider God's many promises to provide for us.

We find the first two lessons in the following quotation from the gospel of Matthew. First, Jesus warns us of the foolishness of trusting in money. Money can never give us true security because it can be stolen and destroyed. There is no place where it can be kept completely safe. Second, it is not possible to serve both God and money because we cannot serve two masters. It is not that money itself is evil. Money can achieve many good things if it is used wisely. It is not sinful to have money, but it is sinful when our time and attention is spent on acquiring money instead of serving God.

> Matthew 6:19-21, 24: "[19] Do not store up for yourselves treasures on earth, where moths and vermin destroy, and where thieves break in and steal. [20] But store up for yourselves treasures in heaven, where moths and vermin do not destroy, and where thieves do not break in and steal. [21] For where your treasure is, there your heart will be also . . . [24] No one can serve two masters. Either you will hate the one and love the other, or you will be devoted to the one and despise the other. You cannot serve both God and Money."

Third, at the end of the parable of the Rich Young Man, as quoted below, Jesus warns us that it is hard for a rich man to enter the kingdom of heaven, possibly because there will be a conflict between serving and trusting in God and depending on and looking after our money.

> Matthew 19:23-24: "[23] Then Jesus said to his disciples, 'Truly I tell you, it is hard for someone who is rich to enter the kingdom of heaven. [24] Again I tell you, it is easier for a camel to go through the eye of a needle than for someone who is rich to enter the kingdom of God.'"

Fourth, in the parable of the Rich Fool, Jesus describes a man who spent his time and attention on building up wealth and possessions that he could not take with him when he died, rather than spending any time preparing for his eternal destiny. He had served money, but he had not served God and faced dire consequences as a result.

> Luke 12:15, 20-21: "[15] Then he said to them, 'Watch out!
> Be on your guard against all kinds of greed; life does not consist in
> an abundance of possessions.' . . . [20] But God said to him, 'You fool!
> This very night your life will be demanded from you. Then who
> will get what you have prepared for yourself?' [21] This is how it will
> be with whoever stores up things for themselves but is not rich
> towards God."

Fifth, Jesus' teaching in the Beatitudes, as recorded by Luke and quoted below, is even more severe than those written by Matthew. This brief passage shows how the rich will face God's justice: if we have enjoyed wealth and comfort on earth, we have already received our reward and so will not be comforted later.

> Luke 6:24-25: "[24] But woe to you who are rich, for you have already
> received your comfort. [25] Woe to you who are well fed now, for you will
> go hungry. Woe to you who laugh now, for you will mourn and weep."

Sixth, in the parable of the Rich Man and Lazarus, Jesus confirms His warning given in the Beatitudes: those who are rich now will not receive any reward later. He also confirms that it is difficult for us to serve both God and money, for this rich man had spent his time building up personal wealth and had not helped others, nor served God. His destiny was eternal suffering, like the Rich Fool who we considered earlier.

> Luke 16:24-26: "[24] So he called to him, 'Father Abraham, have pity
> on me and send Lazarus to dip the tip of his finger in water and
> cool my tongue, because I am in agony in this fire.' [25] But Abraham
> replied, 'Son, remember that in your lifetime you received your
> good things, while Lazarus received bad things, but now he is
> comforted here and you are in agony. [26] And besides all this,
> between us and you a great chasm has been set in place, so that
> those who want to go from here to you cannot, nor can anyone
> cross over from there to us.'"

Finally, Paul also warns us of the danger of spending our time acquiring wealth instead of serving God. He confirms the lesson taught in the parable of the Rich Fool: we cannot take our wealth with us when we die. He adds two further warnings: first, the love of money is the root of evil which can lead to ruin, destruction and to our being led away from the faith. Paul also warns us that the love of money can steal our joy. If we love money, we will always want more. In direct contrast, happiness comes from being grateful and content with what we have.

> 1 Timothy 6:6-10: "⁶ But godliness with contentment is great gain. ⁷ For we brought nothing into the world, and we can take nothing out of it. ⁸ But if we have food and clothing, we will be content with that. ⁹ Those who want to get rich fall into temptation and a trap and into many foolish and harmful desires that plunge people into ruin and destruction. ¹⁰ For the love of money is a root of all kinds of evil. Some people, eager for money, have wandered from the faith and pierced themselves with many griefs."

The Bible also teaches us the importance of recognising where our provision comes from. Whatever money we have has been given to us by God and we should give generously towards His house, the church, in recognition that we are only stewards of the money which God has so generously given us.

> James 1:17: "Every good and perfect gift is from above, coming down from the Father of the heavenly lights, who does not change like shifting shadows."

In the passage from Malachi, quoted below, we find God speaking some very strong and challenging words. In verse 8, He is accusing the Israelites of robbing Him and in response the Israelites asked how they had robbed Him. The fact that the Israelites are being accused of robbery implies that they were stealing something which belonged to God. Under Old Testament Law, God had told the Israelites that the first 10 per cent of their grain, fruit and livestock belonged to Him and was holy. By withholding their tithes, they were stealing from God and were under a curse.

There is no command to tithe in the New Testament and opinions differ as to whether Christians should tithe. Certainly, we are no longer under the Law.

Many people believe that a tithe is the very least that we should give. The New Testament does include many passages about giving and the blessing promised to those who give generously. This chastisement in the Old Testament is followed by five wonderful promises, promises which will be given to those who ensure that God's house is well provided for. I believe that these promises can also be applied to us.

> Malachi 3:8-12: "[8] 'Will a mere mortal rob God? Yet you rob me. But you ask, "How are we robbing you?" In tithes and offerings. [9] You are under a curse – your whole nation – because you are robbing me. [10] Bring the whole tithe into the storehouse, that there may be food in my house. Test me in this,' says the LORD Almighty, 'and see if I will not throw open the floodgates of heaven and pour out so much blessing that there will not be room enough to store it. [11] I will prevent pests from devouring your crops, and the vines in your fields will not drop their fruit before it is ripe,' says the LORD Almighty. [12] 'Then all the nations will call you blessed, for yours will be a delightful land,' says the LORD Almighty."

Having considered the dangers of having a wrong attitude to money, let us now consider some of the passages which promise God's faithful provision when we are generous. In fact, the Bible uses two different phrases to describe this principle: first, Paul speaks about "sowing and reaping" and in other passages the Bible speaks about "giving and receiving". The verb "to sow" indicates an investment. We sow seeds to receive a harvest, or we invest into a business to gain financial benefits. The verb "to give" indicates a donation made for the benefit of others. It is not made specifically to receive a reward. However, many passages promise that giving will also produce generous rewards in our lives. Jesus also confirms the principle of giving and receiving as quoted in the verse at the beginning of this chapter: the measure that we give will determine the measure which we receive.

Let us first consider two passages in which Paul speaks about the principle of "sowing and reaping". In the first passage he applies this principle to finances and in the second to moral behaviour.

We all understand this principle of sowing and reaping when it is applied to agriculture. There are three lessons that we can learn from doing so: first, if we want to receive a harvest, we must plant some seed. Second, the size of our harvest depends on how many seeds we plant. Third, if we plant wheat seeds, we will receive a harvest of wheat but if we plant thistle seeds, we will receive a harvest of thistles. We all understand and accept these three truths when we apply them to agriculture. For some reason, we find it hard to apply these same truths to our lives: we want to receive financial or material provision without first giving to God's work or to others and we believe that we can think, speak, and act in a negative way without it producing destructive consequences in our lives.

We find this principle taught clearly in two passages. The first is in Paul's first letter to the Corinthians and the second is in his letter to the Galatians, both quoted below: we will reap according to how we sow. First, when we sow little, we will reap little. Second, when we give generously, we will have all that we need and have enough for every good work. Third, when we act according to our sinful nature, we will reap destruction in our lives.

> 2 Corinthians 9:6-8, 10-11: "[6] Remember this: whoever sows sparingly will also reap sparingly, and whoever sows generously will also reap generously. [7] Each of you should give what you have decided in your heart to give, not reluctantly or under compulsion, for God loves a cheerful giver. [8] And God is able to bless you abundantly, so that in all things at all times, having all that you need, you will abound in every good work . . . [10] Now he who supplies seed to the sower and bread for food will also supply and increase your store of seed and will enlarge the harvest of your righteousness. [11] You will be enriched in every way so that you can be generous on every occasion, and through us your generosity will result in thanksgiving to God."

> Galatians 6:7-8: "[7] Do not be deceived: God cannot be mocked. A man reaps what he sows. [8] Whoever sows to please their flesh, from the flesh will reap destruction; whoever sows to please the Spirit, from the Spirit will reap eternal life."

Jesus' words, as quoted at the beginning of this chapter, also confirm this principle of "sowing and reaping" and "giving and receiving" very clearly. He tells us that the measure that we give will determine the measure that we receive. How is it, then, that we think that we can hold on to what we have and then expect God to provide for us?

In the Old Testament, we find the dramatic demonstration of this truth in the story of the Widow of Zarephath. We find this story in 1 Kings 17:8-16. She had only a handful of flour and a little oil which she was about to use to prepare a last meal for herself and her son. However, when she followed Elijah's instructions and baked a small cake of bread for him, providing this meal for him first, Elijah and her household were able to eat for many days. This widow was facing dire circumstances: she did not have enough food for herself and her son, but when she gave what little she had to Elijah, God multiplied it and made it enough for them all for many days. Later in this chapter, I will tell an up-to-date story which is very similar to this one.

Paul's letters also include passages confirming God's promise to provide for us when, and only when, we are generous to others. In his second letter to the Corinthians, chapter 8 and verses 1-4, he commends the Macedonians who had been going through a most severe trial and who were also facing extreme poverty, and yet they had pleaded to be allowed to give towards the needs of fellow believers. Paul continues in the following chapter, chapter 9 and verses 1-8, to refer once again to the generosity of the Macedonians and promises that God will ensure that they always have enough for every good work because they have first given to others out of their poverty.

In his letter to the Philippians, chapter 4 and verses 14-20, Paul repeats a similar promise that God will generously provide for their every need, but only because they had entered into partnership with him and had been generously supporting his gospel ministry right from the beginning, even when other churches had not done so.

We find three further confirmations of the benefits of giving in the book of Proverbs: first, if we give generously we will prosper, and when we help others we will be helped. Second, if we share our food with the poor we will be blessed. Third, if we give to the poor, we will not lack anything but if we fail to help the poor, we will be cursed.

Proverbs 11:24-25: "[24] One person gives freely, yet gains even more; another withholds unduly, but comes to poverty. [25] A generous person will prosper; whoever refreshes others will be refreshed."

Proverbs 22:9: "The generous will themselves be blessed, for they share their food with the poor."

Proverbs 28:27: "Those who give to the poor will lack nothing, but those who close their eyes to them receive many curses."

It is possible for us to exempt ourselves from the need to give because we consider ourselves too poor. However, there are no legitimate reasons to disqualify ourselves from this biblical principle. There are three reasons why this principle applies to every one of us: first, in the Old Testament story of the Widow of Zarephath and in Paul's reference to the Macedonians, both of which we considered earlier, people gave generously even when they did not have adequate supplies for themselves. Second, our generosity does not depend on the amount that we give but on its proportion to what we have. Jesus confirmed this when He commended the widow who put two small copper coins into the temple treasury. He said that she had given more than those who had put in large amounts because it was everything that she had. Third, we all have something that we can share. If we do not have any money at all, we can share clothing, or food, or a practical skill.

These principles of "sowing and reaping" and "giving and receiving" both confirm that we are not helpless victims who are dependent on the help of others. In direct contrast, our destiny is largely determined by whether we choose to be generous, even when we do not have enough for our own needs. It confirms this wonderful truth that we really can give our way out of poverty. This is what Lameck did with his clothing. His family had very little but when he shared some of it with his friends in Mozambique, God sent me to Malawi and enabled us to send them about one million articles of clothing over the following thirty years.

I have also experienced several examples of this principle. Several years ago, two of us visited Malawi when one of our container consignments arrived in Blantyre. We were therefore present when some of this clothing was distributed. We do not normally do this as we consider it rather patronising and lacking in trust for us to be organising the distribution. Also, local pastors know who are in most need. Even during this trip, we were purely observers and did not get involved with giving out any of the clothing.

Most of our trips at this time included daily visits to different churches and so we took some boxes of clothing with us so that we could distribute them to the congregation at the end of each service. We never advertised these distributions as it would result in a multitude of people wanting to receive something, leading to a difficult and even dangerous situation. After about three days of visiting different churches, the word had obviously got around that we were distributing clothing because on the following day we found about 1,000 people waiting for us instead of the normal congregation of about 150.

After the service, the church leaders who had accompanied members of their congregations to this meeting, together with the leaders with whom we were travelling, were uncertain what to do as we only had eight boxes of clothing and these would not go very far with such a large crowd. We waited for some time while these leaders discussed the situation. After a while, they decided to proceed with the distribution. Several of the leaders stood holding the crowd back from where the vehicle and the boxes of clothing were. Each church leader had brought a list of their congregation members with him and so one by one the leaders read out these names and each person walked forward to receive some clothing when their name was called.

This process took some time and each person was given two garments. Everyone present received clothing and when the distribution was finished there were four boxes which had not even been opened! Bearing in mind that each box would not have held more than about fifty garments, I believe that we witnessed a very similar miracle to that of the provision of food for the crowd of 5,000, as told in the gospels.

I was also told of a story which is very similar to that of the widow of Zarephath. There was an area pastor in Malawi called Benson Chale. Sadly, he died recently. Lameck told me that there was some quite serious flooding in Mozambique about fifteen years ago and a group of church members came across the border to Chinsomba Village where Pastor Chale lived, looking for hospitality. Pastor Chale testified that he only had half a bag of maize flour when they arrived and did not therefore have enough food to feed all these people. However, each day, his wife took flour out of this bag to cook for his visitors and the level did not go down until after they left about one month later.

This same pastor shared another story of God's care for them as a family. He had inherited some cows from his father and had sold some of them to raise finances for the church. Apparently, the next time his female cows gave birth, many of them produced two calves instead of one, thus replacing the ones that he had sold.

Dan Nkhandwe, who is a church leader and pastor in Malawi and who also oversees our projects, testified that he was distributing bags of maize flour during a time of drought when more people were waiting at the distribution point than he had expected, and he knew that he did not have enough bags for each of them. However, he took the faith step of distributing the flour and had enough for everyone.

More recently, Lawrence Msamange – one of Lameck's sons – told me another story of God's wonderful provision for him. Apparently, he had a jacket which he really liked. One day, one of their pastors was visiting his house when he felt that God was asking him to give this much-loved jacket to his visitor. He found this a challenging request and shared that he went into his bedroom several times to collect the jacket but came back without it. After several failed attempts to obey this prompting of the Holy Spirit, he gave the jacket to his friend.

About one week later, Lawrence went to the airport to meet a friend who had been travelling abroad. As his friend approached, he was carrying a large box. He told Lawrence that he had a present for him but that he should not open it until he got home. You can imagine, perhaps, what was in the box: a brand-new jacket!

I shared this story at a very recent church meeting in Malawi, and the area pastor for that area followed this story of Lawrence's jacket with his own story. It was while he was studying in Bible school that he had felt challenged to give his only jacket away. However, a few days later he was unexpectedly given a sum of money which was enough to buy two jackets!

Finally, as a charity, we have continued to send both funds and relief consignments to Africa for over thirty years without asking for any donations or fund-raising in any way and we have never had a bill which we could not pay and the donations keep arriving with wonderful and amazing regularity. Surely, God is wonderfully good and faithful to us when we apply His principles to our lives.

Chapter 15

Life in the Villages

1 Timothy 6:6-10: "[6] But godliness *actually* is a means of great gain when accompanied by contentment. [7] For we have brought nothing into the world, so we cannot take anything out of it either. [8] If we have food and covering, with these we shall be content. [9] But those who want to get rich fall into temptation and a snare and many foolish and harmful desires which plunge men into ruin and destruction. [10] For the love of money is a root of all sorts of evil, and some by longing for it have wandered away from the faith and pierced themselves with many griefs." (NASB)

During my early travels in Tanzania, I had worked primarily with the Anglican Church and so when I visited these churches, church leaders arranged for me to stay either with missionary families who were working with the church or in a few cases with the bishop himself. In all these situations, therefore, I was staying in a European-style house with all modern conveniences.

When I first wrote to Lameck about visiting Malawi, I had asked if I could stay with him. However, due to him missing me at the airport and my going to the Grace Bandawe Guest House, it was agreed that I would continue to stay in this same guest house. I did this for the first fifteen months until God spoke very clearly, asking me to sleep in the villages with the local people. I discussed this with Lameck who said that this would not be possible because no Westerners ever sleep in the villages. I said that as God had asked me to do this, He would also enable me to do it. Lameck therefore agreed and I spent my first night in Kampomo Village in the autumn of 1988, sharing my small room with a broody chicken!

This challenge to sleep in the villages turned out to be extremely significant. I learned later how much it meant to local people that I, and later others, were prepared to spend time with them, sleeping in their houses, using their toilets and eating their food. It made them feel valued as individuals and gave us a better understanding of the severe limitations of their circumstances, and later to fund projects which were both appropriate and beneficial.

We stayed in the villages whenever we travelled down to the Lower Shire for many years until Peter Guta developed diabetes and needed to keep his insulin in a refrigerator. We were then forced to stay in guest houses where there would be electricity and a refrigerator. I have to confess that while we were staying in the villages, I did try to make myself a little more comfortable by taking a thin camping mattress with me and making myself a thin cotton sleeping bag – which was more suitable for the intense heat – and also a cotton quilted pillow case with a zip which I could fill with my folded clothing and use as a pillow.

There are very few brick buildings in the Lower Shire and most of their houses are constructed of mud and thatch. A timber frame is constructed first and then mud is taken from ant hills and coated on both sides of the timber, rather like the wattle and daub of sixteenth-century houses in the UK. They use mud from ant hills as the ants have secreted a sticky substance into the mud so that it adheres together.

Some houses are made from mud bricks which are made by pushing clay soil mixed with a little water into a mould, then removing the clay bricks from the mould and leaving them in the sun to dry. A few houses will be constructed using these mud bricks which have been burnt to make bricks which are like those used in the West. They do this by stacking the mud bricks to a height of about six to eight feet, leaving several small triangular holes at the base, lighting fires in these holes, covering the bricks with a layer of mud on the outside and leaving them in the heat for about three days.

Most houses, especially those constructed of mud, are small and square. They usually have a veranda outside the only entrance and small windows which have shutters to reduce the invasion of mosquitos. Glass would be too expensive and unnecessary because the weather is hot. These buildings are therefore very dark. Few houses would have any furniture of any kind and clothing is hung over pieces of string which are strung across some of the rooms. They may occasionally have a table and chairs, but these would be rare, and most families would eat sitting on bamboo mats with the food placed in the centre. They would have a wooden door for the main entrance but the inside doorways would only have a piece of material hanging from string.

They also sleep on these same bamboo mats with no mattress or pillows. Several children may sleep on the same mat with one room for the boys and another for the girls. They do not make a bed with sheets as we would in the West, but simply wrap a sheet or blanket around them.

There is no electricity or running water. All water is collected from either a village well, if they have one, or from a nearby river – which would be contaminated from animals drinking from it and people washing themselves and their clothing in it. Collecting the water is a job that is always performed by women and children, and the water is carried on their heads in large metal buckets or clay jars and this can produce spine damage.

Women collecting water from rivers also face the problem of crocodiles who are present in the rivers and who will often attack them. Over the years I have heard of several women who have been killed in this way. Added to this, during drought, families can be reduced to collecting "nyika" (water-lily bulbs) to eat from the bottom of rivers and women have also been killed by crocodiles while diving down to the bottom of rivers to collect these bulbs for food. (This reminds me of the stories of the Dutch being reduced to eating tulip bulbs during the Second World War.) This happened recently when Pastor Harrison's daughter and a friend were killed, and a third lady was seriously mauled and needed extensive skin grafts to her legs. Hyenas and hippopotamuses can also kill people. In 1996, Area Pastor White Simente was killed by a hippopotamus who, being hungry, came into the villages looking for food.

Not every family would have a toilet. Many defecate on the open ground where excrement can be washed into the rivers, producing further contamination. If families construct a toilet it will be a pit latrine with either a mud and thatch construction over it, like their houses, or one made of bamboo. They do not have any doors to their toilets which are entered by a narrow corridor into an inner chamber with a simple open hole.

There is no toilet paper although you do sometimes find some torn newspaper inside. I have learned to take a small packet of paper hankies and a torch with me when I visit the villages. Sometimes the toilet can be a little way from the house and one concern I had was to find the right house to return to if I used the toilet during the night as all the houses look very similar, especially in the dark!

Every member of the family will wash themselves each morning in an African-style shower room. These are normally constructed of bamboo but can occasionally be constructed of brick. Once again, they do not have a door and you enter through a narrow corridor into a centre chamber where the wife will put a metal bucket filled with water and a mug with which you can pour water over yourself. Clothing and towels are hung over the walls. If it happens to be raining, this clothing will get wet as there is no roof.

In most villages, the houses will be built in the centre with the land around them used for their gardens. (Each family is dependent on growing their own food to eat.) Some more wealthy families will have several buildings in a compound with one building for the adults, another for the children and a third as a kitchen store. The area around the houses is kept clear to discourage snakes from entering the houses and at 6am each morning you can hear the ladies sweeping this area clean.

There will be several other buildings and structures in a village. As families are subsistence farmers who are dependent upon growing enough food for their families, they will build granaries in which they can store their crops for use throughout the following year. These can be either round or rectangular and are usually made with a wooden framework which is interwoven with bamboo. They will have a thatched roof which lifts off and legs to keep the contents off the ground to stop vermin from eating their crops.

They will also construct either structures or compounds for some of their animals. Cows will be kept overnight in a compound which is surrounded by thorn branches. Young boys will take these animals out during the day to forage for food. Goats will be kept in a kraal overnight. These can be constructed of either brick, wood or bamboo. Goats are left to forage freely throughout the day without any supervision. Cows and goats are expensive and only owned by a few families.

Poorer families may have a variety of other animals such as pigs, chickens, pigeons and guinea fowl for eating, dogs to guard their homes and cats to kill the mice.

Cooking is done outside, except when it rains. Ladies cook on the ground using three stones on which they rest their cooking pots with firewood pushed between these stones. It must be a back-breaking job and the inhalation of smoke can cause serious problems with their lungs. At night the only source of light will be the flames under the cooking pots which must make seeing the contents very difficult.

Most church buildings are constructed of mud and thatch like their houses. However, they face difficulty in thatching the wide span of the roof. Some will be built with mud bricks and a few with burnt bricks and a corrugated iron roof. The corrugated iron is, however, expensive and more than most congregations can afford. At many of the meetings that we attend, we will meet under a tree, even if they have a church building, so that there is room for surrounding village congregations to join us. I admit that I prefer this because in the intense heat, it is cooler to be outside.

The inside of church buildings is usually very basic. They will either construct benches and a lectern of mud or the congregation will sit on bamboo mats. Once again, the windows will be small, and they may construct a toilet outside the church.

Baptisms are done in rivers or shallow muddy streams. Because of the rapid growth of most churches, several people will be baptised at the same time – sometimes this can be as many as 150 people at one time. Once again, there is the potential problem of crocodiles but with the large number of people present, these rarely cause a problem as they will usually only attack either individuals or small groups. However, it takes a brave pastor to stand in a crocodile-infested river for perhaps an hour baptising so many people!

Funerals are a common feature in the villages, and everything will stop, even important planned meetings, for a funeral. They seem more numerous because of the large number of people who will attend them. Normally a whole village will participate in each funeral and so families would attend far more funerals than would be normal for us in the West. They also last much longer as most will take about twenty-four hours from beginning to end. With no funeral parlours, village members will prepare the body, make the coffin, dig the grave and carry the body to its final burying place.

I have attended many funerals over the years, and they are very moving occasions. Funerals are usually held within twenty-four hours of death because they have no way of keeping the body cold. When a person dies, women will immediately walk around the whole village wailing to announce the death. Upon hearing the wailing, families will start to make their way to the dead person's house where they will stay all night, accompanying and comforting the bereaved family. They will stay awake all night singing while close family members will sit or lie close to the coffin, often wailing to show their grief.

The following morning, men will go to dig the grave and, for Christian believers, the first service will usually be held outside the dead person's house. After the service is finished, the coffin will be carried to the burial place, which may be some distance away and is usually in a wooded area where the body will not be disturbed. Everyone will accompany the coffin on foot, singing all the time, and with men taking it in turns to carry it. When they arrive at the burial area, they will hold another service. At Christian funerals, the gospel message will be preached boldly, and many people will respond to the altar call before the body is put into the grave. The coffin will then be lowered into the grave, the dead person's sleeping mat laid on top of the coffin and the hole filled with soil. Ladies will then come and cover the grave with flowers and the funeral ends.

Africans will demonstrate their grief loudly and visibly, but this does not continue after the funeral. (There are several New Testament passages describing a similar behaviour.) In many ways it is perhaps better to express our grief rather than suppressing it and suffering later because we have not allowed our emotions the freedom of being expressed.

Because all central African countries are near the equator, the sun rises and sets at about 6am and 6pm throughout the year. As they have no electricity, families would therefore rise with the sun and go to sleep early. They do use kerosene lamps but the fuel would be expensive and so they would only be used sparingly.

I have many memories of the time spent in various villages in the Lower Shire. Some were more challenging and others humorous. I will finish this chapter by sharing a few of these.

Two of these memories occurred in Maglasi Village. Four of us had made this trip: Jay Ainge – a trustee of Faith in Action; Frank Scammell – an Anglican minister; Charles Croll – a United Reformed Church minister; and myself. We spent about ten to twelve days in this village. (We would usually travel around and only stay in each village for about three days.) Pastor Morishu Makala and his wife very graciously gave us their house to sleep in and they slept elsewhere. This is so typical of African hospitality. This house had one reception area and two other rooms leading off it. Frank and Charles were given one room, Jay and myself the other.

Although this visit was during the dry season, it did shower during our time there and this gave us an insight into the difficulties faced in a village when it rains. The thatched roof was not thick enough and so the rain came through it where there were thin areas and made our bedding and clothing wet. We thought about how difficult this would be in the rainy season when the rain would be far heavier, and we were told that families sometimes need to stand throughout the night because of the rain coming through the roof. It is also difficult to wash because their wash rooms do not have a roof and I have heard stories of people falling into their latrines when the floor joists become damp and collapse with the weight of someone standing on them. During this trip, we did hear one cry from the latrine when Charles' spectacles nearly fell out of his pocket and down the hole where they could never have been retrieved!

One evening, Jay and I went into our room to sleep when we saw a mouse running around the room. Our immediate concern was that it would run into one of our sleeping bags, which were laid out on the floor, and from where it would be far more difficult to remove it. We therefore tried to chase the mouse out of the room at the same time as attempting to stop it running into these sleeping bags. Frank and Charles heard the noise from their room and over the next few days teased us about our supposed fear of mice. We felt justice was done a few days later when we heard a cry from their room when a frog jumped down from the rafters onto one of their beds!

Ruth, our daughter, and I faced a similar situation during a different trip. I do not remember the name of the village. On this occasion we were given a new house to sleep in, not knowing that new houses will not have dried out and can attract frogs who like the damp. (I am not afraid of mice, but I do confess to a fear of frogs.) We awoke on the first morning to find a frog hopping round our room. We discussed how we could remove it as neither of us were keen to pick it up. I remembered the way that my mother used to catch spiders with a glass and a piece of paper pushed underneath it. Frogs, however, are heavier and larger than a spider. I remembered that I had an empty plastic ice-cream container with my wash things in it. I therefore emptied it and put it over the frog while I tried to find something that I could push underneath. I thought that its lid would be too thick. Meanwhile, the frog continued to hop around the room with the ice-cream container bobbing up and down with the frog! Not finding anything else, I managed to push the plastic lid under the base, and we were able to lower the frog through the back window!

One very eye-opening situation happened during another trip when I travelled with a member of my church. She told me later that she had been watching the ladies prepare a meal for us. They had been cutting up some cabbage, ready for cooking, when some thin shivers of cabbage had fallen on the sandy ground from where some children had picked it up and eaten it. I could not help thinking of the stark contrast between so many Western children who dislike even nicely prepared and cooked cabbage eaten off a clean plate and these children who were pleased to eat uncooked and sandy cabbage off the ground.

Staying in the villages has certainly been a challenging and instructive experience. We can often take so much for granted in the West and sometimes consider that we have a right to live in relative luxury while millions of people throughout the world live their entire lives struggling to survive on a day-to-day basis. Amazingly, I have found more joy and contentment in Africa than I see amid all our comparative luxury in the UK. It is not what we have that makes us happy, but what we are grateful for, and when we believe that we have a right to something, we are rarely grateful for it.

Chapter 16

"I Was Hungry and Thirsty"

Matthew 25:34-36: "[34] Then the King will say to those on his right, 'Come, you who are blessed by my Father; take your inheritance, the kingdom prepared for you since the creation of the world. [35] For I was hungry and you gave me something to eat, I was thirsty and you gave me something to drink, I was a stranger and you invited me in, [36] I needed clothes and you clothed me, I was ill and you looked after me, I was in prison and you came to visit me.'"

Matthew 10:40-42: "[40] Anyone who welcomes you welcomes me, and anyone who welcomes me welcomes the one who sent me. [41] Whoever welcomes a prophet as a prophet will receive a prophet's reward, and whoever welcomes a righteous person as a righteous person will receive a righteous person's reward. [42] And if anyone gives even a cup of cold water to one of these little ones who is my disciple, truly I tell you, that person will certainly not lose their reward."

It was in September 1988 that we started to fund development projects in Malawi with the provision of funds for three poultry projects. Over the following years this small beginning has grown to include funds for a large variety of development projects, Christian resources, legal support, training, transport and medical needs.

The growth in development projects has been driven by the tremendous need that we have found throughout the Lower Shire. As I explained in an earlier chapter, this area is triangular and is separated from the rest of Malawi by a thousand-metre escarpment on its northern side. The area is flat and at sea-level in height. It is surrounded on two and a half of its three sides by high mountains. All this means that they often face extremes of weather. When the country experiences insufficient rain, it is hotter and drier in the Lower Shire. When there is too much rain, surface water runs down the escarpment and fills up the area rather like a basin. There have been many times during the last thirty plus years when this has happened so quickly that families have almost no time to escape the water and often climb trees to reach the only place of relative safety.

I have been told two especially harrowing stories. The first was about a lady and her small baby. She had climbed a tree to escape the flood water and had stayed there for three days holding onto her baby because the flood-water had not gone down. Eventually her arms became so tired that she dropped the baby into the water, and it was swept away.

The second story happened during 2015 when the whole area experienced the worst flooding that we have seen during the last thirty years. I was told by a person who witnessed this event that in one village the people ran to higher ground to escape the water, but as the level rose, the area where one group were standing became surrounded by water and formed an island from which there was no escape. Crocodiles then approached this area and killed all of them. I was also caught up in some serious flooding in 1989 but I will tell this story in the following chapter.

The fact that we had been staying in the villages has enabled us to choose projects which are appropriate for their needs, circumstances and climate. Also, because we have focused our time and attention on this one church and have stayed with local pastors during our visits to Malawi, we have been able to build very strong friendships with church leaders and to work as a team with them, deciding together how best to respond to each crisis that they face. We have never funded any project that has not been fully endorsed by local people and this has certainly been an important factor in their success. Nobody is likely to maintain something which they do not want.

However, we have also faced major setbacks and delays which have been caused mainly by extreme weather conditions. On several occasions, many of our projects have been swept away by flood water. There was one occasion when very heavy rains caused villages to be covered to a depth of about ten to twelve feet with eroded soil – it being sandy – and a few wells which we have provided to be buried as well as their houses. Working in Africa is not for the faint-hearted who can be tempted to give up following such destruction or who only see their ministry to this country on a short-term basis!

In concluding this chapter, I will describe four of our projects which provide communities with food and water. In doing so, I will be writing about practical issues which may appear to be outside the remit of this book. However, I believe that it shows the extent to which God has continued to extend and to diversify our ministry in ways beyond anything that I could have imagined at the beginning. It also shows how much He cares about every aspect of our lives. I will describe other spiritual and practical areas of ministry in later chapters.

First, let us consider the provision of clean drinking water. It is one of the most essential requirements that we all share as human beings. However, although most of us in the UK take this basic provision for granted, there are millions of people in other countries who do not have access to clean drinking water.

During years of drought, women may have to walk for six hours to find water which they have to carry home on their heads, causing neck and spine injuries. Furthermore, this source of water will be contaminated because people wash themselves and their clothing in rivers and animals also drink there as well. Further pollution is caused because not every family will build a latrine and so they will defecate on open ground from where this excrement will be washed into the rivers. The provision of clean drinking water will significantly reduce the large number of deaths which are caused by diarrhoea in developing countries. I read one report which stated that 5,000 children die every day from drinking dirty water.

We have learned that it is important to use the appropriate process for building these wells and thus we ensure that local people are involved in every stage of drilling each well. This local involvement produces recognition of ownership and thus responsibility to service and maintain each well. Before any drilling work is started, the development co-ordinator will meet with representatives from each village to discuss where they would like the well to be built. This site is then checked with government workers and a committee is formed to take responsibility to look after the well and some of these committee members will be trained to service the pump. We use Afridev pumps because spare parts are available in rural village markets.

Second, let us consider three projects which bring about greater food security. Most families in the Lower Shire are subsistence farmers who are dependent on growing enough food each year to provide for all their needs. However, weather patterns have changed, and much suffering has been caused during the last twenty years from unreliable rains. Although there have been a few years when excessive rain has caused flooding, the greatest problem has been caused by insufficient rain.

To overcome the serious problem caused by poor rains, we have provided loans to construct wind-pump irrigation systems. Nine of these had to be replaced following very serious flooding in which these systems were destroyed. (Part of many of these systems were funded with the loan repayments.) The irrigation systems which we have used have all been manufactured in Malawi and so spare parts, as well as the technology to maintain the equipment, are available locally.

These wind-pump irrigation systems provide a low-technology, easy to maintain, free to run, way to bring about greatly increased food security. As they draw water up from a well, they can be set up throughout the Lower Shire and not just beside a river as with many other methods of irrigation. They are also better for the environment as they circulate ground water instead of taking water from rivers.

These irrigation systems will not only enable farmers to grow a more reliable crop each year during the rainy season but also a second crop during the dry season. If flooding destroys crops during the rainy season, farmers can grow a replacement crop during the dry season when it is unlikely to flood.

Each irrigation project is provided as an interest-free loan which provides funding for constructing an irrigation system within the village together with accountancy training, seeds, fertiliser, sacks, stationery and transport. The loan for this community project is given with an agreement from the farmers – who benefit from the irrigation – to sell half of their crops and to give the proceeds for community projects within their local area. (Fifty per cent of two crops is the same as, or possibly more than, 100 per cent of one which has often failed because of unreliable rains. They may also benefit from the community projects.) The loan will be repaid in four payments after each harvest is sold. These loan repayments will be used to set up further irrigation projects.

We encourage communities to use the net income from their first harvest to build a community centre. When this building has been completed, part of the income from the following harvests can then be used to set up and run an orphan day-care centre in this building.

There are a vast number of orphaned children in Africa, many – but not all – orphaned because their parents have died from AIDS. To give just two examples of the scale of this problem: in Jimu Village there were 220 families and 500 orphans and in Chambuluka Village there were 250 families and 600 orphans. Sadly, many orphans only have grandparents to care for them and this poses a very heavy financial and physical burden on elderly people. Area Pastor Arone Mpomba and his wife were both in their seventies when Pastor Mpomba died in 2008. They had had ten children, seven of whom had died, and twenty-three grandchildren for whom they had been responsible.

These orphan day-care centres will give appropriate help to these grandparents. The children will be cared for and fed by paid staff during the day and will return to their grandparents at night. In this way the family relationship, which is important in African culture, is maintained while the physical and financial burden is taken off elderly people. It will also provide employment for some people living in the village.

We have also provided goats for younger families who have taken in orphaned children. Each family is given one male and two female goats. Each female goat should produce two kids twice a year and if all these kids are sold, this sale should produce an annual income of about £250. (This would be a significant sum for a village family.) However, if families choose to keep one of their female kids each year instead of selling all of them, they can build their stock of breeding females and increase their yearly income. If they do this each year, they can receive a yearly income of over £1,000 by the tenth year. The provision of goats will also provide much-needed protein for the family.

After the loan for the irrigation system has been repaid, there should be enough income to set up other projects in the local area as well.

These irrigation projects therefore enable communities to not only provide food for themselves, but also to become donors providing a whole range of benefits for village members.

During a visit to Malawi in 2017, we learned that wind speeds had increased in recent years and this had been causing damage to these wind-pump systems, costing them an increased amount to maintain them. Farmers have therefore asked if we could provide solar-powered systems instead. The solar-powered irrigation systems are more expensive than the wind-pump systems, but they irrigate 200 acres of land instead of just 50 acres.

Each of our current wind-pump irrigation systems irrigate 50 acres of land but solar-powered systems will irrigate 200 acres of land. Consequently, 100 acres will be used to grow crops for the farmers' personal use and the crops from the remaining 100 acres will be sold to raise funds for local projects. Two crops of soya beans, Masika maize and groundnuts grown on 100 acres of land should produce an annual net income of about £100,000. This amount should transform communities.

Towards the end of 2013, we set up a second farming project with two main aims: first, to encourage farmers to work together in groups in order that they may buy seeds and fertiliser and to sell their surplus crops at better prices. Second, to introduce better farming methods and to encourage students to share this teaching with other farmers who live in the villages around them.

A group of nine farmers attended a "God's Way of Farming" course. The main aim of this course is to teach farmers how to conserve rain water, to stop soil erosion and to increase their crop yields through the following techniques: first, farmers are taught how the conventional method of preparing their fields through digging over the whole area encourages soil erosion, especially as their soil is sandy. Second, instead of digging over the whole field, farmers are taught to dig a hole where each plant is to be sown. Third, fertiliser is then added to the base of each hole. In this way the fertiliser is concentrated where it will benefit the plants the most. Fourth, seeds are then planted in each hole and covered with soil. Fifth, a thick layer of mulch is laid over the entire area. This mulch can include any fibrous vegetative material and provides two important benefits: it stops the sun from drying out the soil and rain will be absorbed into this mulch layer, draining slowly down into the soil below, instead of running off the cultivated area and eroding the soil in the process.

At a meeting held in 2017 with six of the farmers who had attended this course, they reported that this method of farming had doubled their yields and that they had been able to teach this new method of farming to many farmers in their communities when they saw the increased yields that it produces.

The third very cost-effective farming project is to provide a variety of more drought and flood-resistant crops. The main staple crop grown in the Lower Shire is maize. However, local maize is very dependent on good rain, takes 135 days to mature and produces a poor yield. Over the past twenty years this crop has repeatedly failed due to a change in local weather patterns. Providing a variety of crops which can be planted in rotation in their fields will also reduce the risk of spreading disease. Furthermore, soya beans and groundnuts both have the extra benefit of adding much-needed protein to their diet. They are also nitrogen-fixing crops which will increase the fertility of the soil.

Over recent years we have been providing funds for the following crops: first, plantain bananas, which look like normal bananas but their fruit is different. The skin of a plantain needs to be cut off with a knife and the inner flesh is then cooked and eaten as a staple food. It is not a fruit. The stem of a plantain is thick, unlike the thin stem of maize, and its roots go deeper into the soil. Consequently, the plant is less likely to be flattened during flooding or to dry out when there is too little rain. Each sucker will produce one hand of plantains after six to nine months. It will also produce three suckers which can be shared with other farmers.

Second, cassava is a tuber which is produced by the roots of the plant. It is white like a potato, but its texture is crisp like a carrot. Cassava can be eaten raw or cooked whole. It can also be processed into a flour and cooked as a thick porridge. Cassava is a drought crop which can be planted as a second crop after their normal crops are harvested. It can therefore substantially increase the amount of food produced each year. It needs to be planted while there is still some moisture in the soil. However, once it has been planted, it will grow without further rain. Each plant should provide three cuttings which can be shared with other farmers.

Third, Masika maize is a variety of maize which matures in almost half the time of local maize, produces a higher yield, and requires less rain. The plant takes 75–85 days to mature and therefore compares well with local maize which takes 135–145 days. Consequently, if the rains stop early it is possible to produce a crop of Masika maize when local maize would fail. One acre of Masika maize should produce a yield of 3,000–4,000kg of cobs and this compares very well with local maize which has an estimated yield of only 400–600kg.

Fourth, soya beans have four benefits for farmers. First, they have a high protein content which is especially valuable in an area where protein consumption is very low. Second, they can be grown as a cash crop. Both soya beans and groundnuts have an extensive international market and can be sold for high prices. Third, soya beans and groundnuts are nitrogen-fixing plants which will increase the fertility of the soil.

We have suggested that farmers grow an acre of soya and then sell three-quarters of their crop, leaving one quarter to add protein to their own diet. With the high price paid for the soya, they should be able to buy maize with the income gained and have considerable funds left over.

Fifth, groundnuts have the same benefits as soya beans: first, they have high protein. Second, they can be grown as a cash crop. Third, they are nitrogen-fixing plants which will improve the fertility of the soil.

Sixth, millet is a traditional crop that was grown in the Lower Shire before the introduction of maize. Farmers stopped growing millet when they discovered the better flavour of maize. However, weather patterns have changed in the Lower Shire and the local maize has often failed over recent years. Many farmers now want to grow crops which will provide them with greater food security. Millet takes 90 days to mature which compares well with local maize which matures in 135–145 days. It also requires less rain than local maize.

Seventh, we also provide fertiliser. The benefits of fertiliser have not been understood in the Lower Shire and it is not traditional for farmers to use it. However, after we had provided some fertiliser for several villages in November 2007, local pastors told us with great enthusiasm that one acre without fertiliser would produce only five to thirty 50kg bags of Masika maize, while one acre with fertiliser had produced fifty-five to seventy bags. Having seen its significant benefits, families are now motivated to use fertiliser in future and want to encourage other farmers to do so as well. Funds gained from the increased yields should provide farmers with income to buy their own fertiliser for the following years.

All these four projects have been well received by local people and have provided significant benefits for communities.

Chapter 17

Out of My Comfort Zone

Matthew 28:18-20: "[18] Then Jesus came to them and said,
'All authority in heaven and on earth has been given to me.
[19] Therefore go and make disciples of all nations, baptising them
in the name of the Father and of the Son and of the Holy Spirit,
[20] and teaching them to obey everything I have commanded you.
And surely I am with you always, to the very end of the age.'"

Working with the Faith in Action Church in Malawi has been the most amazing adventure. It has stretched me far beyond my comfort zone. I am not courageous, but I have been working with a group of people who are both courageous and absolutely committed to building God's Kingdom at any cost, as explained in a previous chapter when I shared about Lameck risking his life to take Bibles into communist Mozambique. I have therefore accompanied them on many trips that I would never have chosen to make myself because I was only too aware of the difficulties that we could face.

However, facing repeated difficulties has built my faith as I have seen God constantly care for us, protect us and rescue us. It is when we are prepared to go out on a limb that we see Him act in such magnificent ways and it is in the difficult situations that people are more open to the gospel because they recognise their own very limited ability to cope with the circumstances which they face.

It would be difficult to give a detailed account of the last thirty-one years because so much has happened. During this time I have learnt much about the paradox of the gospel, so many aspects of it being the very opposite to what our natural senses and the world would tell us. In this respect, I have found that it is often easier when the circumstances are harder because God simply picks us up and carries us. It is, perhaps, only when we run out of our own resources that we fully abandon ourselves to His care.

I have seen so many wonderful demonstrations of God's faithful love and care. I will share some in this chapter and others elsewhere. We saw a very visible miracle on a visit to the eastern side of the Lower Shire. The weather was very hot, and we had been sleeping in Chambuluka Village while taking our meals with a nurse in Trinity Hospital about two miles away. Each morning and evening we had to walk from one location to the other in the full sun. This nurse had lent me her umbrella to protect me from the sun but on the last morning I returned the umbrella to her. She said that I could keep it and return it to her later so that I could walk back to the village with it, but I knew that it would be some time before it could be returned to her and so I left without it. Amazingly, there were no clouds that day except for one extremely small one which followed us back and shaded me all the way to the village. For some time after this event, this story was shared from village to village and it was referred to as "Sally's cloud".

God has rescued us from numerous car break-downs, far too many to describe them all. Perhaps the most common problem was with punctures. Because the tyres were usually almost bald, these happened on a very regular basis. Often, they happened twice on the same day so that we did not have a spare. Travelling in African villages is very different from the UK. There are very few garages and in the early years no telephones either. (Many people now have mobile phones, but this was not the case before the turn of the century.) Despite these limitations and without any exceptions, some unforeseen event resolved every situation.

One unusual resolution happened while I was still staying in the Grace Bandawe Guest House, I had met three doctors who were staying there while they worked for three months in the Queen Elizabeth Hospital in Blantyre. They told me that they had already spent about two months in Malawi but had only been able to see the tourist areas of the country. They expressed a desire to visit a village. I therefore spoke with Lameck and we arranged to take them to the Lower Shire for the day. The previous day, we had a problem with the car and so Lameck had borrowed another vehicle from a friend.

On route to the first village, we had a puncture and after we had retrieved the spare tyre from the boot, we found that this car did not have a jack. Lameck suggested that we look for a stone which was large enough to lift the side of the car onto so that we could change the tyre. Unfortunately, all the stones that we found were too small except for one very large one which was too heavy for even two of us together to move, let alone lift. Miraculously, one of these doctors was a weight-lifter and he was able to lift this stone single-handedly and carry it to the car so quickly that we were able to change the tyre much faster than if we had been able to use a jack!

We survived another potentially dangerous situation when the brakes on our vehicle stopped working just as we reached the bottom of the escarpment. Because of the continual travelling up and down this steep thousand-metre escarpment, the brake-pads were continually wearing down and, on this occasion, had not been replaced when they should have been. If these brakes had stopped working just a very short time earlier, the result could have been fatal.

There have been other situations from which God has miraculously rescued us. I will share just two of these, both of which exposed fears originating from my childhood, feared situations from which God rescued me and later completely set me free.

I travelled to Malawi alone in February 1989. This was my first time to visit the country during their rainy season – and I hope the last! It was the second visit after God had spoken to me about sleeping in the villages. As virtually all the roads in the Lower Shire at that time were mud, heavy and continual rain can cause very serious difficulties when travelling by car. We had planned to spend about ten days travelling around the Lower Shire and to stay in three different villages.

Our first destination was Dausi Village on the north-western side of the Lower Shire, just south of the escarpment. This village is a long way from the main central tarmac road and can only be approached by a road which is bordered on the southern side by a river and on the northern side by the escarpment. This road was therefore the only way in and out of this area. Although the rains had been normal for this time of year prior to our travelling down to the Lower Shire, once we had left, they increased dramatically and were to cause considerable damage and destruction during the two weeks of this trip.

As I have already mentioned in an earlier chapter, when it rains hard, surface water from the high plateau runs down the escarpment causing considerable trouble in the Lower Shire. We therefore came to a place during our journey to Dausi Village where water running down the escarpment ran over the road. At that time this river was about 24-foot wide and about 18-inches deep so that even in our small vehicle we were able to cross it without too much difficulty. However, Lameck commented that if the rain got worse, which it did, we would not be able to cross it on the way back.

It was not long before we reached the village. We were to stay in one of a group of houses owned by the chief's son and we were given the house that would normally be used by his children. We planned to stay there for three days. As we arrived in the village, it was getting dark. We were welcomed warmly but almost immediately it felt as if an invisible black cloak had been thrown over my shoulders and that it was pushing me down towards the ground. I started to panic. I had never felt such extreme fear before and so this was a new and very frightening experience. I felt very alone even though I was not.

When we were later designated our rooms for the night, I was given an inner room – probably to protect me – which could only be accessed through another room which was also designated as a bedroom. As the pit-latrines were outside, this meant that I could not visit the toilet during the night without walking through this other room where people would be sleeping. My anxiety increased. I started to shake with what seemed an inappropriate and irrational terror.

I now understand that I was experiencing a panic attack which was caused because I was locked up as a punishment when I was a young child. (I do not remember this, but my father told me later that they had resorted to this form of punishment – possibly on a regular basis.) I had always known that I did not like being shut into small spaces, but I had never experienced such extreme fear before. Three aspects of this situation made it more extreme than any that I had ever faced before: I felt very alone, I was staying in a village situation which was very new to me, among people I did not know and from which our departure could be considerably delayed, and I was sleeping in a room which I could not easily get out of. Added to all this, the flooding got much worse and we were to stay in this situation for ten days. There seemed to be no way of escape. I did not get to sleep until about 3am and then only slept briefly.

The rain became so severe that the use of a car during our stay was impossible and we walked to different villages on foot, sinking into the mud which splashed up to our thighs. One of these visits to different villages also required us to wade through a thigh-deep crocodile-infested river because the canoe that had been arranged for us did not arrive.

On the second night, I asked if we could exchange rooms so that I could sleep in the outer room and this helped a little. Miraculously, after three days we were able to drive out of this village and we travelled to Maglasi Village which is located towards the centre of the Lower Shire. Once again, reaching this village was difficult because of the state of the roads, and access to it was across a small stream without any bridge, meaning that it could also be difficult to leave this village. We stayed there for three days before travelling to Chambuluka Village on the eastern side of the Lower Shire. Once again, access to this village was by a road that passed between a river and the escarpment and therefore appeared to be the only way in and out of this area.

As this visit continued, the rain became more and more severe. On the second night after we arrived in Chambuluka Village, we were awoken during the night by people seeking refuge. They had walked from Makhanga Village where the water was now about 5-foot deep. Where we were staying was a little higher and therefore dry, but it meant that one way out would be on a road that was covered by 5-foot of water. My fear and panic therefore continued throughout this trip. It was the night-time that I found most difficult – partly because it was dark and partly because, as the only woman in the team with whom I was travelling, I was alone.

The rain continued. Eventually, we came to the day on which we had planned to leave. We said our goodbyes and loaded our small car, planning to travel in the opposite direction to Makhanga Village, which was flooded. There were several places on this route where the water running down the escarpment ran across the road and we had to drive through water that was about 18-inches deep. After a short while we were passed by a man on a bicycle who said that the bridge over a larger river ahead of us had collapsed and that there was no way out in that direction. It seemed as if we were trapped!

Lameck said that there was a mud road up the steep escarpment which he would never use during the rainy season but that it was now the only possible way out. We turned around and made our way back to where this road started. It was like the roads that I had driven on in mountainous countries like Norway and Switzerland, twisting and turning with sharp bends and a sheer drop on one side of the road, but only single-track and made of mud! It was still pouring with rain and as we constantly got stuck in the mud and had to get out to push the car, we were soon soaking wet and splattered all over with mud.

About one third of the way up this escarpment, we came to a place where the rain had washed half the single-track road away. It was not therefore wide enough for the car to pass. Lameck suggested that we walk to the nearby village to borrow hoes with which we could remove some soil on the inner side of the road, making just enough width for the car to pass. We all got out of the car except for Lameck, who was driving. Walking across this narrow section of road was not difficult but it must have been a very scary experience for Lameck to drive across it. I even considered, very selfishly, removing my luggage from the boot of the car as I was convinced that I would never see it again!

It took us six hours to complete a journey that should only have taken ninety minutes. I have never been so pleased to arrive anywhere as I was when we arrived in Blantyre. Lameck's wife, Rebecca, must have been shocked when we arrived barefoot, soaking wet and covered with mud! I thought that this was the worst experience that I had ever faced but even worse was to follow many years later. If I had not already arranged to visit Malawi with a friend about two months later, I wonder whether I would ever have returned. Lameck commented later that if we could survive that situation together, then we could overcome anything. Certainly, I believe that this difficult trip bonded us together as a team in a way that is not achieved in more normal circumstances.

These panic attacks were to continue whenever I faced situations from which escape was difficult before God completely delivered me from them many years later. Unfortunately, there were to be many occasions when, for different reasons, I found myself in a village with no apparent way out. These situations were extremely difficult, and I will describe a second one.

I had been asked to speak at a three-day seminar in Nsaliva Village. This is a very remote village about ninety minutes' journey from the main central road and with no transport coming anywhere near this village. While we did this, Lameck went into Mozambique with a visitor from America.

We had planned three meetings each day, starting on Friday and finishing midday on Sunday. As the worship alone at each meeting lasted for at least one hour and I was speaking for a second hour, by Saturday evening I was very tired. During Saturday, Benson Kaisi – our driver – drove to Blantyre where he spoke to Lameck's wife. She told him that Lameck's vehicle had broken down and that he should drive to the Mozambican border the next day to collect them.

When Benson returned to Nsaliva and shared what had happened, my heart sank. We were due to drive home after lunch the following day and we would not be able to do so because there would be no vehicle. We had no telephone contact and so we could not ask anyone else to come and collect us and I was due to fly home on the Tuesday. I started to panic.

My anxiety led me to ask if I could miss the Sunday morning meeting and leave with Benson. They all said that they would really like me to stay and to speak. As Benson was due to leave about 4am the following morning, I knew that after I had gone to bed there would be no way out of the village. God spoke to me very clearly and said: "The reason that you are feeling so anxious is because you have not surrendered your will to Me in this matter!" I gulped! It took me about ten minutes to come to the point where I could honestly say, "Lord, I surrender myself to You in this situation." The moment I did this, a wonderful peace descended on me and I went to bed.

About ten minutes after I got into bed, an almost new four-wheel-drive vehicle drove up to the little house where I was sleeping and parked outside my window. It was about midnight. We soon learned that a church leader who had stayed in Blantyre because his step-brother was very sick, had sent this car to collect us because his brother had died, and he wanted us to return for the funeral which was to be the following day. We quickly got dressed, packed up our belongings and left after about fifteen minutes!

All the time that I had been panicking, this car had been driving towards us. In this case, God's will had been for us to leave much earlier, rather than later! The lesson that I learnt from this is that surrendering to God's will had brought about a wonderful peace.

It was many years later in 2015 that God completely delivered me from these childhood fears. The whole year was extremely difficult. It started with sickness, the nature of which caused me considerable anxiety, and this led to extreme sleep deprivation and even more anxiety. Emotionally, I just spiralled downwards and came to a place where I could see no way of escape. I was forced to face so many fears but in this painful process, I was completely set free from them. The following year, I had such a deep sense of God's love for me personally and a joy that completely defied the difficulty of some circumstances that I was facing. Life since has been wonderful. I feel so free and ecstatically happy. This year was dreadful, but the results have been awesome.

Not only has God rescued us from so many difficulties, dangers and car break-downs, but we have also seen wonderful miracles of church growth. (I mentioned in an earlier chapter that the church has grown from fifty to about one thousand churches in thirty-one years.) I will conclude this chapter by sharing just three of these events which brought about significant growth, two of which showed God's unique and unexpected way of drawing people to Himself.

The first happened during our journey back to Blantyre, as I have already described earlier in this chapter. You will remember that we travelled home along a steep mud road in the pouring rain and that the car kept getting stuck in the mud. Fortunately, local people nearly always came to help us to push the car. At one point in the journey we passed through a small town where the road was especially steep. Being a town, many people came to our aid.

I was told later that one of these men could not understand why a "white woman" who was soaking wet and splattered with mud was pushing a car in quite a remote area of Malawi. Apparently, he asked several people who I was and eventually spoke to someone who could answer his question. As a result, he invited church leaders to come and to preach in that town where there was no church, and as a result a church was started there. Lameck has told me recently that they have a group of churches in that area now.

When I share this story, I often say that when we discuss ways of bringing people to faith in the UK, I doubt whether anyone would suggest pushing a car up a steep muddy slope in the pouring rain as a way of building God's Kingdom! God's ways are certainly different from ours and much more effective.

The second event took place in Ntchalo. There is a large sugar plantation there and we had stopped on route to a village meeting to look at this plantation. We met with a small group of men and started to talk to them. They explained that they were from a nearby village, but because of a planned extension of this sugar plantation, they were being forced to move to another location which was far less fertile than their present village and they were not being given enough compensation to re-build their houses. They added that they were in the process of collecting money so that they could hire a lawyer to seek justice for their community.

They did not ask for any financial help, but I felt prompted by God to contribute towards the expense of a lawyer. I asked Lameck whether this would be appropriate, and with his encouragement gave them the Malawi Kwacha equivalent of about £10 sterling. Lameck went on to explain that we were a local group of Christians and that we had a church in a nearby village. He gave them the name of the pastor of this church.

I heard later that they were so surprised and encouraged by my very small contribution to their fund, that they had visited this pastor and had asked him to come and preach in their village. Many of them were converted and eighteen months later there were three churches in this area, each with a congregation of about 150 people, all the result of this one very small gift.

Who would not give just £10 to bring almost 500 people to faith?

The third event was, perhaps, less dramatic. Following one two-week visit in which we held a seminar in one of the villages and attended about three funerals, several pastors who had attended these events approached Lameck to ask whether they could join the Faith in Action group of churches. I was told later that they had been so impressed with the purity of the gospel as presented in the seminar, together with the fact that I had attended these funerals – it is not usual for Europeans to do so – that led to their decision to join us. Many of these pastors had a group of churches that they had set up and thus a total of 201 churches joined us after this two-week visit.

When we walk with God, depending on Him and allowing Him to act, the results are amazing. I am reminded, once again, of John the Baptist's words after he had baptised Jesus. Certainly, as I have got to know God better, I find myself doing less and Him doing more.

John 3:30: "He must increase, but I must decrease." (NASB)

Chapter 18

Gender Issues

Proverbs 31:10-12: "[10] A wife of noble character who can find?
She is worth far more than rubies. [11] Her husband has full
confidence in her and lacks nothing of value. [12] She brings him
good, not harm, all the days of her life."

Having travelled quite extensively around Africa, I have found that women have not been greatly valued in this society. In many cases, the church is trying to bring about change but traditions which go back perhaps hundreds of years are hard to break. The situation is changing in the larger towns, but in the rural areas, the traditional way of thinking and acting is more deeply rooted. The traditions and experiences that I will describe in this chapter relate mainly to my experience of working extensively with one church in southern Malawi. Other churches and countries may be different. However, having travelled throughout East Africa, I consider it very probable that these traditions may be found more widely.

Scripture makes it very clear that the role of men and women is different, but every individual is equally loved and valued by God. Scripture also teaches us that men have been given a position of authority in the home, but with authority comes responsibility. We cannot take responsibility for anything if we are not also given authority. However, if we have been given a position of authority, we will also be held responsible to care for every person under our authority.

I really liked the melody of one song that was being sung in the church in Malawi until it was translated for me. Apparently, the words translated from Chichewa into English were: "If you love Jesus, you will not beat your wife in church!" I wonder whether it was inferring that it is OK to beat her at home! I understand that this song was written to correct an incident that happened in one church meeting.

Writing about my experiences with one church in Malawi, we have seen significant change in the attitudes and behaviour of men towards their wives, and this has been very encouraging. Thirty years ago, if you were to take a photograph of a husband and wife, they would stand about 4-foot apart, almost as if they did not know each other and you would never see a man showing any affection towards his wife, not even to hold her hand. Also, if you have a meal with any family, the men of that household might join you, but the women would always stay in the kitchen, sitting on the floor with the children.

At any kind of group meeting, it was traditional to introduce a visitor to everyone else present but only the men were introduced, the women were ignored. This has now changed within the churches with which we are linked. In these churches it is now common, when each man stands to be introduced, for him to ask his wife to come and to stand with him. He may then put his arms around her shoulders and say how beautiful she is. This is a huge cultural change and is nearly always accompanied by loud clapping and cheering from everyone. The church is therefore changing, but in my limited experience, traditions outside the church have not.

Another fact which concerns me is that women rarely play any role within the church except to cook meals during conferences and after meetings where the village has received visitors. I would very much like to encourage women to run a separate meeting on Sundays for children who are usually left to attend the adult service.

Many years ago, I was asked to speak at a three-day seminar on marriage. I certainly did not feel qualified to do so, but I felt that God was asking: who would do it if I did not? I spent some time looking at biblical teaching on this hugely important subject but also spoke about the physical side of the relationship as well. Once again, I discovered the destructive nature of some of the traditions that were destroying these relationships and that there was very limited knowledge about how this relationship should be enjoyed by both husband and wife. Their positive response to this teaching has changed and enriched so many marriages. One pastor shared how after he had applied some of this teaching, thus enabling his wife to enjoy their relationship more, she had started to heat his water to wash in, instead of giving him cold!

There are two other local traditions in Malawi which have far more serious consequences and which the church is struggling to stand against for both are in serious conflict with Christian teaching. Both relate to traditions that are practised after a husband dies. There is still a lot of witchcraft practised in the rural villages in Malawi and many of these traditions are aimed at appeasing their ancestral spirits. It is therefore common, when a husband dies, for a male relative to force a sexual relationship on his bereaved wife to appease these ancestral spirits. This is, of course, not only morally and spiritually wrong but it also increases the spread of AIDS as well.

It is therefore true that there are many women in churches who not only face bereavement, but who are also surrounded by non-Christian male relatives, all forcing their traditions and sexual attentions upon them. As I wrote earlier, the church is now learning to stand with her and to protect her, but this is causing a serious conflict between Christians and non-Christians. We went through a period in Malawi when many church buildings and pastors' houses were being burnt down because the church was growing fast, and this was thought to be making each village vulnerable to spiritual attack because their traditions were not being upheld.

The second tradition faced by a bereaved wife, is for the non-Christian relatives of her husband to take all their possessions from her, leaving her with nothing. This would include houses, finances, animals and possessions. Women are esteemed so lowly that male relatives consider that they have the right to everything. However, we should perhaps remember with shame that it was not so long ago in the UK that a similar attitude prevailed towards women. I watched a documentary about Queen Elizabeth I, saying that one possible reason why she did not get married was because all her possessions would belong to her husband, and it was only one hundred years ago that women were not considered eligible to vote. I also understand that if either a husband and wife have a joint bank account and one of them is rendered incapable of managing their affairs, such as going into a coma, and has not completed a Power of Attorney, their partner is not able to access funds from that joint account and is left without any income to live on.

Several years ago, one of our senior and very committed and faithful area pastors died, leaving a bereaved wife. When I first heard about their story, as

I mentioned in an earlier chapter, Pastor Mpomba and his wife were in their seventies. They had had ten children, seven of whom had died – some from AIDS. The three remaining children were all girls who had married and moved away from their parents. As a result of the death of seven of their children, this elderly pastor and his wife were responsible for the care of twenty-three grandchildren, all of whom had lost their parents.

Almost unbelievably, after the late Pastor Mpomba's death, some of their remaining children and grandchildren came and took their house, leaving their eighty-year-old mother/grandmother with nowhere to live. As a result, she had to move from the village in Malawi where she had lived with her husband and travel into Mozambique where she had family with whom she could stay. As soon as we heard about these events, we provided funds to build her a house back in her home village. Then, in order to protect her from losing this house in the same way, we established that this house was owned by the church and was available for her to live in for the rest of her life.

It was only one year ago that another of our senior and very committed and faithful area pastors died. As I have already shared in an earlier chapter, the late Pastor Benson Chale had inherited a large herd of cows from his father. These cows had provided him with the financial resources to build a brick house for his family which is still quite unusual in this southern area of Malawi. Following his death, his non-Christian relative took some of his cows and said that they would come back for his brick house and the rest of his cows. His wife was therefore not only facing the grief and loneliness of losing her husband, but destitution as well.

As soon as we heard what had happened, we hired a Christian lawyer to meet with her husband's family and to get a restraining order for the return of the cows which had already been taken. Fortunately, the law in Malawi has now changed and a husband's possessions should, by law, pass to his wife and then to his children. Sadly, however, few communities living in the rural areas of Malawi know about this change in the law. On this occasion the late Pastor Chale's family accepted the new law and returned the cows.

We are now planning to train a group of men and women about this new law so that they can travel round the rural areas teaching communities that this dreadful tradition is now illegal and that they could be taken to court and to prison if they break it. For their protection, two people will travel together, and they will seek the local chief's permission, presence and support to hold these meetings. I have also suggested that we teach husbands to write a will in which they make it clear that they want their possessions to be given to their wife, and for a copy of this will to be given to the local chief so that he can oversee the application of it.

I believe that it is important for us to teach a correct biblical view about gender issues because there is still much misunderstanding about it. The biblical view is very clear: both men and women are equally loved and valued by God and both can be equally empowered and fruitful for Him. However, their roles and positions of authority differ in some situations. Attempting to give more detailed and specific information about this highly controversial subject would be outside the remit of the book.

Chapter 19

"I Was Sick"

Matthew 25:34-36: "[34] Then the King will say to those on his right, 'Come, you who are blessed by my Father; take your inheritance, the kingdom prepared for you since the creation of the world. [35] For I was hungry and you gave me something to eat, I was thirsty and you gave me something to drink, I was a stranger and you invited me in, [36] I needed clothes and you clothed me, I was ill and you looked after me, I was in prison and you came to visit me.'"

The needs in Africa can, at times, seem overwhelming. This is especially true when we develop close relationships with our Christian colleagues in this vast continent and get to know them almost as well as we know our own family in the UK. We have consequently faced many situations where we have had difficult decisions to make: do we send funds to provide a project for a whole community or do we use those same funds to save one person's life. Rightly or wrongly, we have usually chosen the latter.

In contrast with the UK, even very serious medical conditions can be treated in a private hospital for a very reasonable price, and therefore – in my opinion – there is no excuse in allowing someone to die when their life could have been saved. I could give many examples of lives which have been saved from various quite advanced cancers, cerebral malaria, meningitis, diabetes, very serious head wounds and severe mauling by a crocodile, to name just a few. However, this decision is always a difficult one and the need to give account for these choices in our regular news-sheets is very important. To date, we have sent over £26,000 for medical treatment.

Visiting an African hospital can be an eye-opening experience! There are very often two patients in each bed with another patient under the bed and ladies – who are there to cook food for their husband or children – sleeping between the beds. The doctors who work in each hospital are few and therefore work very long hours. Medicines and equipment can also be severely limited. Visiting any hospital to pray for those who are sick can, however, be a very rewarding experience from a Christian perspective because everyone is very open to listen to the gospel and to receive prayer.

As well as visiting people in hospital and providing funds for medical treatment, there are three other ways in which we are working to reduce sickness and unnecessary death. The transmission of very common diseases causes serious problems in the Lower Shire and much of it could be easily prevented. There are many reasons why people are vulnerable to disease.

First, not every family will build a toilet and therefore defecate on open ground from where the excrement can be washed into rivers. Second, even those who have a toilet rarely use toilet paper or have any water with which to wash their hands. Third, many families collect drinking water from contaminated rivers. Fourth, flooding brings the effluent from pit-latrines to the surface, from where it contaminates water-sources. Fifth, families have lacked the knowledge of good hand-washing procedures which would reduce the spread of disease.

Our first medical project was to introduce a very successful teaching programme on disease transmission and this teaching has produced noticeable health improvements. This teaching is presented to village communities by voluntary workers who travel from village to village teaching families how to reduce the transmission of disease. This scheme includes the provision of bicycles for these voluntary workers and sets of disease transmission cards which show that if some simple protective steps are not taken, communities can eat the excrement of other people, and it is this which can make them sick. These sets of cards include red cards which show how disease is spread and green cards which show how this spread of contamination can be blocked.

These health cards are laminated A5 sheets, each one with a picture of different disease transmitters (edged in red) and disease blockers (edged in green). There are forty-eight cards in each set, together with two index sheets which show the voluntary workers how these cards should be used. The red disease transmitter cards are given to local people first and they are asked to work out how disease can be spread by laying these cards on the ground to form chains, chains which show different ways that excrement can be passed from one person to the mouth of another.

When these cards have been laid out in the right order, a set of green cards showing different ways of blocking disease are given to the people. They are then encouraged to insert these disease-blocking cards within each chain of cards on the ground so that each chain of disease is blocked. A whole community can participate in the laying out of these cards from children to grandparents and the visual aspect of these cards communicates this teaching in a way that can be clearly understood by everyone.

These cards show seven different ways that disease can be spread. I will describe just two of these. First, a person visits the toilet (red card 1). He gets his hands dirty (red card 2) and goes to eat a meal. Traditionally, each member of the family will use one common bowl to wash their hands in before a meal (red card 3). In this way excrement from the first person's hands is passed into the water and on to the rest of the family (red card 4). As they eat with their hands, contamination is passed from hand to food (red card 5) to mouth (red card 6). This chain of disease is blocked by using a jug to pour water over each person's hands instead of a common bowl (green card 3). We understand that communities throughout the Lower Shire have now changed the traditional way that they wash their hands before meals. This shows, I believe, how some very simple low-cost teaching can save lives.

Second, families who do not have a toilet defecate on open ground (red card 1). Rain (red card 3) washes this excrement into a river from where women collect drinking water (red cards 4-6), which is drunk (red cards 7-8). This chain can be blocked either by building a toilet, or by digging a hole and burying the excrement, or by putting ash from the fire over the excrement (green card 2). (Ash has antiseptic properties.)

Our second medical project is to provide mosquito nets. Benson Kaisi is a member of the church leadership team in Blantyre. Tragically, his four-year-old son, Lewis, died from cerebral malaria in November 2007. We had arranged for him to go to a private hospital for treatment, but he died shortly after his arrival. This tragic incident focused our attention on the fact that many lives are lost from malaria and that these deaths could be significantly reduced by using mosquito nets. Sadly, most families lacked the knowledge, as well as the finances, to protect themselves in this way.

In response to this tragedy, we set up a long-term account in Malawi which pays a very high rate of interest every thirty days, and we use the interest payments from this account to buy mosquito nets. We have also arranged to buy mosquito nets from a local wholesaler who is offering us a competitive price because we will continue to buy nets from them and because the nets will be given to families who could not afford to buy them.

When these mosquito nets are given out, teaching is given about how to use them and care for them. When these nets were first given out, families were delighted as they did not know that they could protect themselves from malaria in this way. They said it was as if they had been given gold. Pastors have also testified that they can now sleep peacefully, and their children do better at school. The current total of our investment into this account is only £10,337, but during the eleven-year period from January 2008 to October 2018, the interest from this account has been used to purchase 10,087 nets which were distributed to 4,015 families in 292 villages. The capital remains intact.

We have also provided over one hundred bicycle ambulances which enable communities to take sick people to hospital. In many villages the nearest hospital may be a long distance away. Traditionally, a seriously sick person would be tied to a chair and carried to a hospital by family members who would usually walk during the evening and night when it is cooler. Because the task of carrying a sick person to hospital can be so difficult, family members will very often delay taking them there until it is too late and thus many people die before they receive any medical care.

Bicycle ambulances are an excellent solution to this difficulty. They make it much easier and quicker to take sick people to hospital from villages where the terrain may not be suitable for cars and cars are very rarely available. sAs well as helping sick people to get medical care before it is too late, the provision of these bicycle ambulances will also lessen the serious risk of spreading disease which is caused by carrying sick people.

These ambulances are made of a welded tubular-metal framework with a mesh of metal strips in the centre. This is covered with a mattress on which the patient lies. The front is attached to a bicycle and the centre is supported by two bicycle wheels. There are two holders for umbrellas which protect the patient from the sun. The ambulance can be separated from the bicycle and pulled by hand when the terrain is especially bad.

Each ambulance is kept with a local pastor who lends it to anyone as the need arises. In this way the church demonstrates God's love to the whole community. The person who borrows the bicycle ambulance signs in a book when he borrows it, and again when he returns it. We understand that these ambulances are on the road day and night because the need for them is so great. They are also used for taking pregnant ladies to hospital for the delivery of their babies, and for collecting dead bodies from hospital and taking these bodies back to their home village for burial.

We have received the following testimony about the significant benefits of these bicycle ambulances. A family in Malemia Village had approached the pastor in Chamboko Village during the night because they wanted to borrow the bicycle ambulance. The husband had cerebral malaria and needed to be taken to hospital quickly. The pastor not only lent them the bicycle ambulance but also got up and went to the hospital with them. When they arrived, a doctor said that if they had come just twenty minutes later the man would have died. Without the bicycle ambulance he would not have received treatment in time. When the man regained consciousness, he asked what had happened. When he heard how they had received help that night, he said that he had never seen such a demonstration of love. As a result, fifteen members of this family have become Christians and have joined the church.

These three projects show that it is possible to significantly reduce sickness and even to save people's lives at relatively low-cost. To give just one example, for the current price of just £15 sterling, it is possible to buy three mosquito nets and protect a whole family from malaria. Let us remember Jesus' parable of the Good Samaritan in which He warns us not to pass by those whose lives we are able to save. He also told us that when we do this for even the very least in society, we do it for Him.

Chapter 20

Let Us Go Deeper

Ezekiel 47:1-6: "¹ The man brought me back to the entrance to the temple, and I saw water coming out from under the threshold of the temple towards the east (for the temple faced east). The water was coming down from under the south side of the temple, south of the altar. ² He then brought me out through the north gate and led me round the outside to the outer gate facing east, and the water was trickling from the south side. ³ As the man went eastward with a measuring line in his hand, he measured off a thousand cubits and then led me through water that was ankle-deep. ⁴ He measured off another thousand cubits and led me through water that was knee-deep. He measured off another thousand and led me through water that was up to the waist. ⁵ He measured off another thousand, but now it was a river that I could not cross, because the water had risen and was deep enough to swim in – a river that no one could cross. ⁶ He asked me, 'Son of man, do you see this?' Then he led me back to the bank of the river."

This well-known passage in which Ezekiel describes a vision given to him by God is frequently said to describe the flow of the Holy Spirit in the lives of new covenant believers, as described many years later by Jesus. It is also suggested that the measuring rod and the different depths of water should lead us to reflect on how deeply immersed we are in the flow of the Holy Spirit.

The person who is walking through water ankle-deep is still very much in control of his life. He can, at any time, decide on what direction he wants to go and is rarely sensitive to the leadings and promptings of the Holy Spirit. In direct contrast, the person who is out of their depth and swimming, is so immersed in the Holy Spirit and so sensitive and obedient to His leadings and promptings that he no longer controls his own life but allows God to guide him on a moment-by-moment basis. God, of course, allows us to choose how deeply immersed in Him we want to be, but this choice will have dramatic consequences in the effectiveness and fruitfulness of our lives.

> John 7:37-39: "[37] On the last and greatest day of the festival, Jesus stood and said in a loud voice, 'Let anyone who is thirsty come to me and drink. [38] Whoever believes in me, as Scripture has said, rivers of living water will flow from within them.' [39] By this he meant the Spirit, whom those who believed in him were later to receive. Up to that time the Spirit had not been given, since Jesus had not yet been glorified."

It is my strong belief, based on experience, that if we want to see God's miraculous power flowing through our lives, we need to be out of our depth. We need to live in a place where we cannot live without Him. This can be very risky and challenging, but wonderfully fulfilling and exciting. Sadly, we often prefer to remain in control of our lives and thus deny ourselves the excitement of seeing God do the miraculous on a regular basis.

Let me try to clarify the kind of life which I am describing. First, let us consider the disciples. In response to Jesus' call to follow Him, they left everything to follow Jesus and were therefore totally dependent on Him. They not only left their homes and families but also their means of earning an income to live on. Throughout Jesus' three years of ministry, they stayed close to Him and were totally dependent on Him. The moment that they responded to Jesus' call, "Follow Me", they were all out of their depth. This fact should help us to better understand the trauma that they must have experienced when Jesus was crucified.

Second, you may remember that in the earlier chapters in this book, I shared about some of the challenges which God presented to us. First, to set up a charity without any plans whatsoever for raising the required funds. Second, to set up a charity without advertising what we were doing or seeking in any way to multiply it. Third, to set up groups packing items for Africa when we had no funds to pay for transport. Fourth, to make a signed agreement with a bank to transfer regular monthly payments to Malawi when we did not have any money or any means of acquiring it. Fifth, to go to Malawi – a country which I had never been to – simply in response to a letter from a person who I had never met and to a group of people I did not know. In all these ways and more, God asked us to do things that we could not do without Him. He has never failed us.

I need to clarify quickly that we should never do any of these things if we do not have a very clear word from God to do them. He has absolutely no obligation whatsoever to provide funds and support for our ideas, however good they may be! He is only obliged to enable us to do those things which He has asked us to do. In an earlier paragraph, I referred to the disciples responding to Jesus' call: "Follow Me." We also need Jesus' directive word before we can step out to achieve things for Him.

There is a New Testament story which describes this process well, and this is when Peter, in response to Jesus' word "Come", steps out of the boat.

> Matthew 14:28-33: "[28] 'Lord, if it's you,' Peter replied, 'tell me to come to you on the water.' [29] 'Come,' he said. Then Peter got down out of the boat, walked on the water and came towards Jesus. [30] But when he saw the wind, he was afraid and, beginning to sink, cried out, 'Lord, save me!' [31] Immediately Jesus reached out his hand and caught him. 'You of little faith,' he said, 'why did you doubt?' [32] And when they climbed into the boat, the wind died down. [33] Then those who were in the boat worshipped him, saying, 'Truly you are the Son of God.'"

There are several lessons which we can learn from this story. First, this is not the only occasion when Peter demonstrated his strong desire to be close to Jesus. Although he later failed to live up to his words, he was the first disciple to promise not to leave or deny Jesus even if it meant dying with Him. Later, when Jesus appeared to the disciples by the lake after His resurrection, it was Peter who immediately leapt out of their boat to reach Jesus on the shore.

> Matthew 26:33-35: "[33] Peter replied, 'Even if all fall away on account of you, I never will.' [34] 'Truly I tell you,' Jesus answered, 'this very night, before the cock crows, you will disown me three times.' [35] But Peter declared, 'Even if I have to die with you, I will never disown you.' And all the other disciples said the same."

John 21:7: "Then the disciple whom Jesus loved said to Peter,
'It is the Lord!' As soon as Simon Peter heard him say,
'It is the Lord,' he wrapped his outer garment round him
(for he had taken it off) and jumped into the water."

On more than one occasion, Peter demonstrated his desire to be close to Jesus and so if we are to learn from this story, we need to consider carefully what our priority is. This is an area where we can very easily deceive ourselves because we so often cover up our true motives with well-used Christian clichés about serving God. We need, therefore, to be brutally honest and face up to the truth about ourselves. If our motivation is to build a reputation and a ministry for ourselves, we are far more likely to attempt to achieve this goal through our own efforts. Afterall, we cannot honestly take credit and honour for something that we have not done. Let us face up to the truth: if we rely on our own efforts, we are unlikely to see a demonstration of God's power.

In direct contrast, when we fall in love with Jesus and desire to be close to Him, our focus will be on Him and not self, and we will take every opportunity to tell others now wonderful He is. We see this with any young lady who falls in love; she will continually bore her friends with details of her young man's many perceived attributes. When we fall in love with Jesus, we will also be prepared to take risks for Him. We will go where He goes and do what He does, regardless of the risk – either to our safety or to our reputation. Like Peter, we will be prepared to get out of the boat, and it is when we are out of our depth that we will see the miraculous, as he did.

Second, Peter asked Jesus to command him to come. He had perhaps come to understand the power of Jesus' words. He had had many opportunities to learn that when Jesus spoke, miraculous things happened, whether it was physical healing, deliverance from evil spirits or the calming of a storm. Like the centurion who believed that Jesus' word was enough to heal his servant, Peter understood that he could only walk on the water if Jesus told him to do so.

Have we learned the same lesson or are we still trying to make our own plans and to achieve things for God through our own efforts? If we want to see God's miraculous power flow through our lives, we need to ask Him to tell us what He wants us to do, and this is likely to include our taking a risk with our personal safety and/or reputation. Let us remember Lameck's preparedness to smuggle Bibles into communist Mozambique. We can aspire to the reputation of another person with a powerful, fruitful and successful ministry, but it will have cost them a great deal to reach the place where they are. Sadly, we often desire their position, but we are not prepared to pay the price that they paid to reach it.

Third, Peter obeyed Jesus' word to him even though obedience would have seemed impossible. We not only need to ask God to lead us, we also need to be prepared to do whatever He asks of us. As I wrote in an earlier chapter, God is not likely to guide us if we are not prepared to obey Him, and this is a sign of His mercy for we will be held responsible for anything that we have heard but not obeyed.

Although obeying God will mean taking risks, we need to remember that His plan for our lives will be tailor-made for us personally. God knows us much better than we know ourselves and He will only lead us according to our interests, desires and abilities. We will therefore find His plan for our lives exciting, rewarding and satisfying.

Furthermore, we may have talents and abilities that we are unaware of and we need God to show us what they are. Only a life spent following Him, will lead to the abundant life that Jesus promised us. If we want to live an exciting, rewarding, satisfying and abundant life, we need to ask what God wants us to do, and then trust that He will enable us to do it.

Fourth, Jesus' one word "Come" was enough. Peter did not need anything else except to keep his focus on that word and on the person who spoke it. There was nothing else which held him on top of the waves. He did not have a boat, a life-jacket or even a piece of wood to cling to. When God gives us His word, He may not immediately provide other resources which would make our obedience any easier. When God speaks, there will always be an assurance that He has done so, but He does not always make the way easy. Jesus' word did not – on this occasion – calm the waves. When God told me to go to Malawi, there was no one at the airport to meet me and no way of contacting the only person whose name I knew in that country. We therefore need to know that God's word is enough and keep our focus on it.

Fifth, Peter was safer walking on the water than the disciples were in the boat. If a storm had arisen, Jesus' word would have held Peter above the waves, but the boat may have sunk. We are always safer close to Jesus than in a perceived place of safety where we are trusting in ourselves or some other worldly security. None of these will give us true security or peace.

It was only recently that God gave me a prophetic word during a church service. The focus of that service was on vision for that year. God told me that He would be leading some members of that congregation to take some risky steps of obedience that year, like Peter getting out of the boat, but they should remember that they will be safer on even the roughest sea than in the false security of a boat.

Sixth, Peter had to get out of the boat before he saw the miracle. God does not perform a miracle until after we have stepped out in faith. If we are waiting for a miracle before we are prepared to take a risk, we will probably wait forever! Let us consider why this is so. Faith is God's currency. If we go into a shop to purchase something, we need to hand over the full monetary value of that object before taking it out of the shop. It is the same with faith. We need to demonstrate our faith before receiving the miracle. Let us remember the many occasions when Jesus told a sick person to perform some act of obedience before they received their healing. I have already shared some of my own experiences of this like walking out of a house with a toilet before God healed my diarrhoea! We see the miracle when we step out of our depth to a place where we cannot survive without God.

Seventh, when we are out of our depth, we are no longer dependent on our own very limited resources and all the unlimited resources of God will be made available to us. All the time that we remain in the boat, we will be very limited in what we are able to do. However, once we step out onto the water, nothing in line with God's will is impossible for us.

If we develop this truth further, all the time we remain in the boat we are likely to be anxious and insecure, knowing that we are relying on our own limited abilities to fix or avoid problems and danger. This insecurity is also likely to increase when we get older and become less able to look after ourselves. However, when we are out of the boat, we will see a constant demonstration of God's presence and care which should build a very deep security in our hearts which cannot be shaken by any storm. Let us remember the contrast between Jesus' peace and the disciples' anxiety when their boat was caught in a storm.

With all these lessons in mind, I need to confess that it was only a year ago when God challenged me: He said that we had settled and become comfortable; we were no longer out of our depth. This was true. Although we had developed exciting new ministries in Malawi, we were only sending the money which we had received. Although we continued to trust God to provide all our finances and were therefore still dependent on Him, we had not committed ourselves to do anything unless we had the necessary funds to do it. Even worse, I could not immediately rectify this problem as I had no clear word to step out on.

The reality of my mistakes slowly became clear. As our work had grown, I had become so engrossed in carrying out the practical and administrative work of our charity that I had been spending less and less time with God and had consequently failed to give Him the opportunity to present us with new challenges. In fact, the truth was even more challenging: our ministry had become so exciting – due entirely to God's wonderful faithfulness – that my focus had shifted onto this and the wonderful people who we were working with, instead of on Him. Although I had always recognised that the honour and glory for everything that we have done is entirely His, I had been finding my fulfilment in the work that He had given me, instead of Him.

Chapter 21

United We Stand

Matthew 12:25: "Jesus knew their thoughts and said to them, 'Every kingdom divided against itself will be ruined, and every city or household divided against itself will not stand.'"

Psalm 133:1-3: "[1] How good and pleasant it is when God's people live together in unity! [2] It is like precious oil poured on the head, running down on the beard, running down on Aaron's beard, down on the collar of his robe. [3] It is as if the dew of Hermon were falling on Mount Zion. For there the LORD bestows his blessing, even life for evermore."

I have learned, sometimes slowly and painfully, that obedience to the many principles taught in God's word results in very powerful and fruitful benefits in our lives. Although Jesus made it very clear that the Christian life would not be easy and that we should expect trials and opposition when we step out to serve Him, life is much better when we humble ourselves and recognise that our more self-centred and self-promoting way of behaving can have very detrimental consequences.

Unity is one of these many principles which can be under-rated and misunderstood despite clear biblical advice on this important subject. I need to confess that it took me many years to learn this lesson. The fact that I was able to get cheap flights to Africa because of Martin's position as a pilot, resulted in me frequently travelling alone. It was easy, therefore, to fall into the temptation of charging ahead without seeing the importance of working closely with other people. God, in His grace, tolerated this selfish behaviour for some years before challenging me about it. He showed me that if I continued to pioneer the work on my own, I would be limited in what I could achieve and showed me the enormous advantages of working in unity with others. I learnt reluctantly to slow down and to share vision with and seek advice from others.

Over the years, I have seen many demonstrations of the amazing benefits of working in unity. It may, at first, appear to make progress slower, but the positive achievements of working in this way are significantly deeper and stronger. Working closely with other people can also protect us from making devastating mistakes. The saying "Pride goes before a fall" is true, and so when we have an inflated opinion of our ability to achieve things through our own efforts alone and fail to submit to and to seek advice from others, we may face very humiliating failure and defeat later. Let us remind ourselves once again of Jesus' warning about pride:

> Luke 14:11: "For all those who exalt themselves will be humbled, and those who humble themselves will be exalted."

God may sometimes allow us to face circumstances where we have no option but to stand alone against opposition and misunderstanding, but these experiences are fortunately less common, especially in countries where the church is not being persecuted. Even in countries where persecution is harsh, God will often provide others to stand with us so that we do not need to face this hardship alone.

I have been very honoured and blessed to work with church leaders in Malawi who lead with humility. We have always worked together as a very close-knit team, and this group has increased in size as area pastors and pastors have become more and more involved in leadership discussions and decisions. Whenever I discuss any matter with Lameck on the telephone, he will always delay any decision until he can discuss the matter with the wider group. This means that every step forward or adjustment that we make always has wide support from members of the church. This unity results in strength and stability and protects us from making some serious mistakes. It also gives everyone a correct biblical view of their value and significance. Furthermore, when we face opposition and testing, we do not have to stand alone.

With the affluence of our Western culture in which we have access to so much excellent teaching and information, we can be tempted to act independently and not to seek advice from our African brethren. Over the years, I have learned that so many Africans have wonderful skills and enormous wisdom, and so we rob ourselves of much significant help if we do not seek their advice. Our strengths and weaknesses will be different and so when we work together, we strengthen each other's weaknesses. Added to all this, it is essential for us to understand local conditions and circumstances if we are to work with local communities in a way that is beneficial and appropriate, and this information can only be given by them.

Over the years, I have taken many people to Africa and with the majority this has been a very positive experience. The only trouble that we have faced has been with those who wanted to act independently and who refused to submit themselves to the church leaders in Malawi. The results of this behaviour made these visits unproductive and very difficult for everyone.

More recently I believe that God gave me a prophetic word in a church meeting about the importance of unity. We were discussing plans to step out into difficult and dark places in our community in the UK. God told me to warn the congregation that such actions would result in considerable spiritual opposition but that we could protect ourselves by being united. He reminded me of the fact that many baptisms in Africa take place in crocodile-infested rivers. I have heard of many people who have been killed by crocodiles as they have collected water or waterlily bulbs (*nyika*) to eat, but I have never heard of any similar attacks during a baptism when many people are present. I have been told that this is because crocodiles will only attack individuals and will not attack a large group.

God spoke to me during that meeting and showed me that we can be protected spiritually when we are united because, like the crocodiles, spiritual forces of evil will tend to attack those who act in an independent way. When we are divided, therefore, through unforgiveness, pride, back-biting, criticism, gossip and slander, we will be especially vulnerable to spiritual attack.

I saw a demonstration of this principle following a friend's visit to Albania shortly after it ceased to be a communist state. You may know that during this communist regime, many Christians were persecuted and slaughtered in that country. Upon his return, he started to have regular dark and disturbing nightmares. He mentioned this during a prayer meeting one

Sunday evening and I felt that God was saying that we needed to stand in a circle around him, holding hands together, and pray a prayer of identification with him. We did this, declaring that we were standing united with him and that evil forces would therefore need to attack all of us; we would not allow our friend to be singled out for we were united. Following this prayer meeting, the nightmares stopped.

Many years later, we saw another wonderful demonstration of the how the presence and power of God is demonstrated when the church is united. As mentioned in an earlier chapter, families in the Lower Shire in Malawi are subsistence farmers and are therefore dependent upon being able to grow their own food. The unreliability of the rain over the last thirty years has therefore caused much suffering and hunger. During the rainy season of 2017–2018, the rain had started well in the beginning of November. During February, however, it stopped for three weeks in the Chapananga district of the Lower Shire, the plants had started to wither and to die, and there was no sign that the rain would start again.

Lameck discussed this situation with me on the telephone and while he spoke, I was reminded of the psalm as quoted at the beginning of this chapter. This psalm tells us that when brothers dwell together in unity, there God commands a blessing. Realising that the rains were still good in the rest of the Lower Shire, I suggested to Lameck that he asked some of the area pastors from this region where the rain was good, to travel to the drought-stricken area to stand in unity with their brethren there. I suggested that these visiting pastors went out into their fields with some local congregations and that they pray, speaking out their faith in this psalm and saying: "Father, You have promised that where brothers dwell together in unity, there You command a blessing. We are standing in unity with our brethren and we are asking for the blessing of rain in this area."

A short time later, Lameck told me what had happened following our telephone conversation. Apparently, several area pastors had travelled to Chapananga and had prayed with local congregations as I had suggested. Following this, they stayed the night in this area before travelling home the following day. As they started their journey home, it began to rain so that they all got wet and it continued to rain solidly in this area for five solid days without stop. Furthermore, when it had traditionally stopped raining in the other areas at the end of March, it continued to rain in this area alone for several more weeks.

During the summer of 2018, God challenged me further about the importance of unity and showed me one area where there was division within us as a team working in Malawi: He explained that this division was caused because some of us considered ourselves to be donors while others saw themselves as beneficiaries. God said that this had to stop for it was divisive and told us that we should all see ourselves as donors. He reminded me of various scriptures and especially the passage in the second book of Corinthians in which Paul commends the Macedonians who had given generously out of their extreme poverty. God also pointed out to me that if the small boy with the five loaves and two fishes – which were far too little to feed that vast crowd – had not given away his lunch, no one would have been fed.

> 2 Corinthians 8:1-4: "[1] And now, brothers and sisters, we want you to know about the grace that God has given the Macedonian churches. [2] In the midst of a very severe trial, their overflowing joy and their extreme poverty welled up in rich generosity. [3] For I testify that they gave as much as they were able, and even beyond their ability. Entirely on their own, [4] they urgently pleaded with us for the privilege of sharing in this service to the Lord's people."

> John 6:8-13: "[8] Another of his disciples, Andrew, Simon Peter's brother, spoke up, [9] 'Here is a boy with five small barley loaves and two small fish, but how far will they go among so many?' [10] Jesus said, 'Make the people sit down.' There was plenty of grass in that place, and they sat down (about five thousand men were there). [11] Jesus then took the loaves, gave thanks, and distributed to those who were seated as much as they wanted. He did the same with the fish. [12] When they had all had enough to eat, he said to his disciples, 'Gather the pieces that are left over. Let nothing be wasted.' [13] So they gathered them and filled twelve baskets with the pieces of the five barley loaves left over by those who had eaten."

I shared these thoughts with the church in Malawi and their response was very positive. They admitted that they had thought that they had too little money to tithe and acknowledged that this was limiting the church in what it could achieve. They also recognised that with over 600 churches in Malawi, even a very small tithe from each family could add up to a sizeable amount. Within a few days they had agreed to open a separate bank account with a bank which had local branches in the Lower Shire, chose four area pastors to be signatories to that account, and planned to use some of the money from that account to provide loans for setting up small family businesses for congregation members. The small interest paid for these loans would further boost the account.

I believe that this dramatic change in attitude will produce many financial benefits for at least four reasons: first, when we are united, God will command His blessing. Second, when we see ourselves as poor and requiring financial support from others, we curse ourselves and block God's many promises to provide for us. In direct contrast, when we see ourselves as a donor, this attitude of faith will open the door to financial provision for us. Third, in a purely practical way, the tithe money will provide much-needed provision for the church. Fourth, as we have already considered in an earlier chapter, the Bible teaches clearly that we will receive in the measure that we first give, and that God will bless those who tithe.

Let me finish this chapter with one more consideration about the importance of unity and this relates to our attitude and behaviour towards other people. When we work closely with others, we communicate love, acceptance and appreciation to and for them, and this is very important because in different passages throughout the New Testament God promises to treat us in the same way as we treat others. We will look at this further in a later chapter. One reason, therefore, why we can often fail to see a demonstration of God's powerful presence in our lives is because when we fail to work in unity with others, we will tend to focus on our own desires and interests and on promoting our own ministry, instead of focusing on and improving the lives and ministry of others and communicating God's wonderful love to them. Unity can be a safeguard against pride and selfishness.

Chapter 22

"I Was in Prison"

Matthew 25:34-36: "[34] Then the King will say to those on his right, 'Come, you who are blessed by my Father; take your inheritance, the kingdom prepared for you since the creation of the world. [35] For I was hungry and you gave me something to eat, I was thirsty and you gave me something to drink, I was a stranger and you invited me in, [36] I needed clothes and you clothed me, I was ill and you looked after me, I was in prison and you came to visit me.'"

Our ministry into prisons started in the autumn of 2010 when God spoke very clearly to me: He said that communities would benefit far more from the development projects which we were funding if they were, at the same time, applying New Testament biblical principles to their lives. He asked me to write some Bible studies based on some of the principles taught in the New Testament. I discussed this with Lameck, who encouraged me to do this and so I wrote them in English and then Wesley, one of Lameck's sons, translated them into Chichewa. I initially thought that we might be able to use a hundred copies, but we have now printed and distributed over 96,000 Bible studies to date.

The writing of these studies was an amazing experience. I quickly learned to carry a pen and paper around with me and to keep them by my bedside when I went to sleep so that I could write notes as thoughts, I believe from the Holy Spirit, kept flooding into my mind.

The Chichewa version of these studies was printed in Malawi with a green border along the top. The first 10,000 copies were distributed on 18th August 2011, when about 500 church leaders met together at Chinsomba Village to receive studies for their congregations. During this launch, Area Pastor Justin Kuleti came to Lameck in tears. He said that about a year ago he had had a dream in which he saw a picture of the Lower Shire, the area where most of the Faith in Action churches are located. He later wrote a testimony of his dream which has been translated into English.

Pastor Justin Kuleti's Testimony: *A year ago, I had a dream which at that time bothered me since I could not understand the meaning of the dream and therefore decided to keep the dream to myself. I dreamt that the whole of the Lower Shire was dry, and every plant and tree was withering, and the situation was pathetic. I could see in the dream that everyone in the Lower Shire was sad and dejected.*

Later in the dream, I saw Sally, Lameck and a few others coming to the Lower Shire with green books in their hands and suddenly everything about the Lower Shire changed. The grass, plants and trees sprouted, and I could see many hands of those who were sad and dejected reaching out to receive these books and this time around, their faces were beaming with joy. I woke up, not understanding the meaning of this dream.

On 18th August, I saw Pastor Lameck and others coming to Pastor Chale's house to distribute green books entitled Living an Abundant Life *and suddenly, I realised the true meaning of the dream. I would like to thank you, Sally, for these studies because now I know that the spiritual dryness is going to be replaced by the spiritual awakening of the Lower Shire.*

On behalf of all the pastors here in the Lower Shire, I praise the Lord who gave you this vision of coming up with these daily studies. Is it possible to get more copies because the ones that we received have already found their way to many hungry souls? Most of our churches in Mozambique are asking for more.

Once again thank you and may the Lord bless you. I had tears of joy the day we received these studies.

Yours, Abusa Kuleti

Following the overwhelming response that we received from the Bible studies that were distributed in Malawi earlier that year, we were asked by church leaders in Zambia, Mozambique and Zimbabwe if they could be translated into their own local languages. To this end, a church member from each of these three countries travelled to Malawi to translate them into Chibemba, Portuguese and Shona. Leaders from at least fifteen other church groups in Malawi have asked if they could have copies for their own churches.

Lameck also had the opportunity to give the archbishop of the Anglican Church in Malawi a copy of these studies. He came back to Lameck two days later and said that he would like every parish and every theological student in the country to have a copy. He added that they would contribute towards the cost of the printing.

We received the following testimony from the Tete area of Mozambique where some of these studies were distributed during May 2013. A man who was observing the distribution of these studies was intrigued because he could see that their cover showed the picture of a church in Mozambique, which is unusual. He asked if he could have a copy. We have been told that he used to take these studies to work and read them during his work breaks. After reading them he, together with six members of his family, became Christians and have been baptised. Apparently, he was well known in the area because he used to drink a lot. We understand that four of his friends, together with their families, have also become Christians after seeing the change in his behaviour.

Pastor Lameck Msamange is not only the founder and leader of the Faith in Action Church in Malawi but he is also a village chief. In this role he is often asked to be involved in government matters and is especially involved with AIDS awareness and prevention.

During one of his visits to the government in Lilongwe in spring 2014, he had the opportunity to speak to a previous president. He asked her if she would like a copy of our Bible studies and she said that she would. However, before an English copy could be given to her, it had to be security checked by the army and while they were checking it, they also read it. As a result, one chief member of the army contacted Lameck to ask for a total of 10,500 copies to be distributed into the seven army barracks in Malawi.

This distribution took place over two weekends in June 2014. Wesley, one of Lameck's sons, sent us an email describing the distribution in the barracks in Zomba. He told us that they were warmly welcomed, and the studies were well received. Many asked for two copies because they wanted one for their spouse or relations. Amazingly, the prison commissioner, based in Zomba Prison, had come to meet his army counterpart to discuss security issues. He asked for two copies of the studies and for Wesley's business card.

Wesley later received an email from him, telling him how two prison wardens directly linked to his office had started to read the studies and asked him to get some more copies to give to their prisoners.

The first distribution of a total of 500 Bibles and 7,860 Bible studies took place in Nsanje and Chikwawa prisons during November 2014. Wesley reported that the prisoners were excited as it was a very rare occasion for them to receive visitors, and the officer in charge thanked the church for remembering them as this was so unbelievable to them. His speech was followed with a loud hand clap and shouts of approval.

The officer in charge called Wesley later to say that the dust still had not settled from their visit because he has sensed a spirit of calm in the whole prison. The prison commissioner contacted Lawrence, another of Lameck's sons, a second time to say that this provision of Bibles and studies had continued to transform these prisons. Wesley and Lawrence also received a letter saying that 103 inmates in Chikwawa Prison had become Christians. They also received requests for Bibles and studies from three more prisons.

During a trip to Malawi that we made at the end of June 2015, we went to visit the prison compound in Zomba. This is the main prison with about 38,000 inmates. We spent about an hour with the prison chaplain who had recently been given responsibility to co-ordinate the work of the chaplains in all the prisons in Malawi. He emphasised, once again, the enormous changes which they had seen in the prisons where prisoners had received these Bibles and Bible studies. He told us that the fighting and violence had stopped, the atmosphere was peaceful and far fewer prisoners were trying to escape. He said that he would like every prisoner in Malawi (1.3 million) to receive a copy of these studies and gave an open invitation for pastors from the Faith in Action Church to visit and preach in every prison.

Over the last four years, we have distributed a total of over 2,400 Bibles and nearly 41,000 Bible studies in Chikwawa, Nsanje, Zomba, Mangochi, Thyolo, Ntcheu, Balaka, Mwanza Neno, Nkhokhota and Muzu prisons.

During spring 2015, Lameck received an unexpected visit from two Mozambican pastors who had travelled 240 miles by bicycle to Blantyre. They had come from an area in Mozambique which is east of Mulanje. They explained that they had come across a copy of one of our Bible studies in Portuguese and, having read the address of the Faith in Action Church on the back of these studies, had travelled all the way to Blantyre to ask for some more copies. Lameck was able to give them some copies of these studies and they asked if leaders of the church would come and visit their area with a view to working together in future. As a result, this group of about eleven churches has now joined the network of Faith in Action churches.

During 2016, Lameck was invited to speak in the daily morning and evening devotional broadcasts for about one month over Easter. He used the Bible studies as the basis of his talks and as a result, he received many telephone calls from both individuals and churches asking if they could buy some of these studies. In response we sent funds to print over 5,800 studies which were distributed to some of the individuals and churches who had asked for copies after these broadcasts earlier that year. Each beneficiary gave a donation towards the cost of printing these studies and this money was used to provide Bibles and studies for another prison.

Later in 2016, the long-term struggle between Renamo (the Portuguese and Catholic-based army) and Frelimo (the communist army) in Mozambique flared up again. During this struggle, Renamo captured and burnt some villages where there were Faith in Action churches. The people there fled in terror. Sometime later, Frelimo re-captured this area and a soldier found one of our Portuguese Bible studies lying on the ground. As a result, a brigadier in the Frelimo army contacted Pastor Golasi, an area pastor in Malawi, asking if they could have 40,000 copies for their army.

In response to this request, we provided funds to purchase over 500 Bibles and to print over 9,000 Bible studies for the Frelimo army in Mozambique. During the distribution, the brigadier who had initially met Pastor Golasi, told Wesley that his father had been a pastor in the Assemblia De Deus (Assemblies of God) church when it was a one-party communist state and Frelimo ruled the country. His father had been tortured and persecuted while preaching the gospel.

He went on to say that at a young age he had joined the army and had gradually risen in rank. He said that he now feels guilty that he never supported his father's ministry or used his rank for God's purpose. Now that his father has been killed, he feels the need to continue his father's legacy through the distribution of the Bibles and Bible studies in the army camps and the promoting of Christianity. He said that as he oversees several provinces in Mozambique, he is strategically positioned to work with the church in the distribution of these studies and to reach out to soldiers because this is the right tool for reconciliation and peace.

Early in 2017, Wesley received a telephone call from a prisoner who was at Ntcheu Prison when he visited that prison during November 2015. He had not been a Christian then and had been arrested for armed robbery. He said that their visit to this prison had been an eye-opener to him and that he spent months feeding on the Bible studies and had accepted Christ. He has now been released from prison and is back in his home village of Manjawira with his family. He said that he and his wife wanted to travel to Blantyre so that they could share his testimony and to request that a church is opened in their area.

During our trip to Malawi at the end of June 2017, we recorded the testimony of a prisoner who was converted to Christ while he was in prison. His name is Moses Ross. He shared the amazing story about how he had stolen a motorbike because he could not feed his family and how Lawrence and Wesley had visited the prison to distribute some of our Bible studies. He shared how he had been convicted and converted to Christ during their visit to the prison and how he was released early because of his transformed behaviour.

He shared how he had received some money from us to start a small business and that he is now able to provide for his family and had also been able to buy the suit which he was wearing. He asked for more Bible studies so that he could go to different prisons to share the good news of the gospel with other men who are in need, as he was.

Later in August 2017, Lameck told me another wonderful story about recent events in Chikwawa Prison. Wesley and Lawrence had distributed Bibles and Bible studies in this prison during November 2014. Apparently, a man who was about forty years old entered this prison a year earlier. He had got drunk one evening and got into a fight with another man; during this fight his opponent had fallen over, banged his head and died. As a result, this man was sent to Chikwawa Prison.

When he arrived, he was given a copy of our Bible studies which he started to study intensely. Following his study, he not only gave his life to the Lord but also started to preach within the prison, exhorting others to read these studies. He has set up a Faith in Action Church Bible Reading Cell in the prison and more and more prisoners are coming to Christ and joining this group. At the time when I was told this story, there were about forty to fifty members.

During November 2017, after considering Jesus' parable of the Wedding Feast in which the master sends his servants out into the highways and byways to invite everyone to this feast, I thought that an appropriate response to this parable would be to hold banquets in prisons in Malawi. One important point in this parable is that we should go into places where other people do not go, to the places where there are outcasts or those who are socially unacceptable and demonstrate God's unconditional love and grace to them.

After discussing this with church leaders in Malawi, we agreed that we would provide prisoners with a meal of chicken with rice, vegetables and fruit; this would be a luxury for them. After the meal there would be a meeting in which they would be told of God's wonderful love for them, even as prisoners, perhaps even sharing this parable and give each of them a copy of our Bible studies together with some Bibles for them to share. We held our first banquet in Nkhotakhota Prison in Malawi on 22nd December for over 2,300 prisoners and their guards.

Wesley and Lawrence travelled to Nkhotakhota Prison with some church members who would assist with the cooking and in the sharing of the food in the different blocks. Wesley reported that this programme was really welcomed, and the prison headquarters had even planned for a witness to be there and to be part of the event. He said that the atmosphere was just wonderful, and they could all sense God's presence in their midst. The excitement on the faces of the prisoners was overwhelming. Even the officers were really looking forward to the meal. They had been told that this is the first time for the prisoners to have chicken in the prison.

The fact that prisoners, officers and the church shared the meal together removed all barriers. There was no longer the element of them and us. They all sat together as God's children. During speech time, one prisoner said this lunch brought back his identity. He had lost all hope, but this gesture of love reminded him of the love of Christ who had died for us. Another said that this was his first Christmas as in the past Christmas was just like any other day.

The officer in charge thanked Faith in Action. She even shed some tears because her many children, as she refers to the prisoners, had received from God through His people. Everyone was so happy to receive the Bibles and studies and some even said that they had heard about other prisons which had received them and so their prayers had been to receive some. Wesley later received word of thirty prisoners who wanted to give their lives to God and so some church leaders based in Blantyre, went for a service to welcome them to Christ. The reason the officer in charge gave for this positive result is that they were so overwhelmed by the love shown by providing the lunch. She said her prayer is for such meals in other prisons, hence reformation taking place in the process.

Following the wonderful success of this meal, we provided a similar meal and Bible studies to the 2,670 prisoners in Muzu Prison the following year, together with some Bibles. We also plan to continue with these meals and Bible study distributions in other prisons as well. Added to this, we have plans to provide funds for teachers to go into the prisons and to teach literacy to those who cannot read and write and to continue to provide loans to set up small businesses for released Christian prisoners.

Over the last thirty plus years, we have also provided a range of other Christian resources in Chichewa. This includes £122,850 for 96,057 Bible studies, £56,017 for Bibles, £2,382 for 127 proclaimers and £6,070 for bicycles, most of which were for pastors. A proclaimer is an audio machine which contains the whole Bible in Chichewa. It can be either solar-powered or hand-wound. The Bibles have been provided through the Bible Society by setting up a standing order with them so that a varied number of Bibles – according to the exchange rate – in a variety of different local languages, are provided each month. On one occasion, Bibles were distributed in one area where eight churches were sharing just two Bibles!

Chapter 23

Praise, a Powerful Weapon

Habakkuk 3:17-18: "¹⁷ Though the fig-tree does not bud and there are no grapes on the vines, though the olive crop fails and the fields produce no food, though there are no sheep in the sheepfold and no cattle in the stalls, ¹⁸ yet I will rejoice in the LORD, I will be joyful in God my Saviour."

Philippians 4:4-7: "⁴ Rejoice in the Lord always. I will say it again: rejoice! ⁵ Let your gentleness be evident to all. The Lord is near. ⁶ Do not be anxious about anything, but in every situation, by prayer and petition, with thanksgiving, present your requests to God. ⁷ And the peace of God, which transcends all understanding, will guard your hearts and your minds in Christ Jesus."

James 1:2: "Consider it pure joy, my brothers and sisters, whenever you face trials of many kinds."

There are so many Bible passages which exhort us to praise God even when we are passing through times of testing and hardship. Just two of these are included at the beginning of this chapter together with the verse from James which advises us to be joyful even during trials. I have learnt from painful experience how very powerful and beneficial obedience to this paradoxical exhortation is. In the natural, it is very difficult and seeming unreasonable for us to remain thankful when circumstances are contrary to our comfort and security. I have learnt, however, that this is the key to living victoriously.

One of the best examples of people who failed to obey this command and suffered as a consequence of their disobedience, is the Israelites as they travelled through the wilderness. We read again and again how they murmured and complained every time they faced hardship or difficulty. Instead of trusting in God's promises to care for them and to take them to the Promised Land, they looked at their circumstances instead of His faithfulness and the many miracles and demonstrations of His presence which they had already seen.

Numbers 11:1-3: "¹ Now the people complained about their hardships in the hearing of the Lᴏʀᴅ, and when he heard them his anger was aroused. Then fire from the Lᴏʀᴅ burned among them and consumed some of the outskirts of the camp. ² When the people cried out to Moses, he prayed to the Lᴏʀᴅ and the fire died down. ³ So that place was called Taberah, because fire from the Lᴏʀᴅ had burned among them."

The Bible records that 603,550 men of fighting age left Egypt, and if women, children and the rest of the men were included, the number would have been significantly greater. Out of this vast number, only two entered the Promised Land. This, I believe, should be a warning to us. We may have started out on our journey of faith, but it is how we finish that really matters.

I would like to consider two biblical stories, both well known, which demonstrate the power of praise and worship. One from the Old Testament and the second from the New. We find the first in the second book of Chronicles, chapter 20. I have quoted below just a short section of this story, but it is well worth reading the whole chapter. Judah was being attacked by the Moabites, the Ammonites and the Meunites during a time when Jehoshaphat was on the throne. Upon hearing that this vast multitude was coming against them, Jehoshaphat focused his attention on seeking God and proclaimed a fast throughout the whole of Judah. The people therefore met together, and King Jehoshaphat cried out to God in a prayer which is recorded in detail and well worth studying because of the many powerful principles included in it.

After his prayer the Spirit of God came upon Jahaziel who gave an amazing word of prophecy in which God gave very clear guidance to the people and promised to give them victory. God also told them that they would not need to fight this battle, for the battle was not theirs but His! What is significant in this passage is that the people took God's word seriously and obeyed it precisely. They believed God when He told them that they would not need to fight and instead of preparing for battle, they appointed those who sang to the Lord to go ahead of the army, and when they worshipped Him, God set ambushes and the enemy was defeated!

2 Chronicles 20:5-9, 14-17, 21-22: "⁵ Then Jehoshaphat stood up in the assembly of Judah and Jerusalem at the temple of the LORD in the front of the new courtyard ⁶ and said: 'LORD, the God of our ancestors, are you not the God who is in heaven? You rule over all the kingdoms of the nations. Power and might are in your hand, and no one can withstand you. ⁷ Our God, did you not drive out the inhabitants of this land before your people Israel and give it for ever to the descendants of Abraham your friend? ⁸ They have lived in it and have built in it a sanctuary for your Name, saying, ⁹ "If calamity comes upon us, whether the sword of judgment, or plague or famine, we will stand in your presence before this temple that bears your Name and will cry out to you in our distress, and you will hear us and save us."' . . . ¹⁴ Then the Spirit of the LORD came on Jahaziel son of Zechariah, the son of Benaiah, the son of Jeiel, the son of Mattaniah, a Levite and descendant of Asaph, as he stood in the assembly. ¹⁵ He said: 'Listen, King Jehoshaphat and all who live in Judah and Jerusalem! This is what the LORD says to you: "Do not be afraid or discouraged because of this vast army. For the battle is not yours, but God's. ¹⁶ Tomorrow march down against them. They will be climbing up by the Pass of Ziz, and you will find them at the end of the gorge in the Desert of Jeruel. ¹⁷ You will not have to fight this battle. Take up your positions; stand firm and see the deliverance the LORD will give you, Judah and Jerusalem. Do not be afraid; do not be discouraged. Go out to face them tomorrow, and the LORD will be with you."' . . . ²¹ After consulting the people, Jehoshaphat appointed men to sing to the LORD and to praise him for the splendour of his holiness as they went out at the head of the army, saying: 'Give thanks to the LORD, for his love endures for ever.' ²² As they began to sing and praise, the LORD set ambushes against the men of Ammon and Moab and Mount Seir who were invading Judah, and they were defeated."

This whole story raises several significant questions. Do we remind ourselves of the wonderful things that God has already done for us as King Jehoshaphat did? Do we stand on God's word when we pray, quoting relevant promises?

Do we take God's word seriously and obey it precisely? Do we believe Him when He promises to do something and change our actions accordingly? Do we understand how the presence and power of God is released when we give Him worship and praise, even in the most adverse circumstances? Are we prepared to step out and to take risks when He leads us to do so?

The second story about praise and worship in adverse circumstances is found in the New Testament. Most of us will know this story well. Following Paul and Silas delivering Lydia from a spirit of divination, the crowd rose up against them, they were beaten with rods and thrown into an inner prison with their feet fastened in stocks. However, instead of bemoaning their situation, Paul and Silas prayed and sang hymns of praise to God. As they did so, a great earthquake shook the foundations of the prison, all the doors were opened, all the prisoners' chains were unfastened, and the jailer asked how he could be saved. What further proof do we need of the power of praise?

> Acts 16:22-30: "22 The crowd joined in the attack against Paul and Silas, and the magistrates ordered them to be stripped and beaten with rods. 23 After they had been severely flogged, they were thrown into prison, and the jailer was commanded to guard them carefully. 24 When he received these orders, he put them in the inner cell and fastened their feet in the stocks. 25 About midnight Paul and Silas were praying and singing hymns to God, and the other prisoners were listening to them. 26 Suddenly there was such a violent earthquake that the foundations of the prison were shaken. At once all the prison doors flew open, and everyone's chains came loose. 27 The jailer woke up, and when he saw the prison doors open, he drew his sword and was about to kill himself because he thought the prisoners had escaped. 28 But Paul shouted, 'Don't harm yourself! We are all here!' 29 The jailer called for lights, rushed in and fell trembling before Paul and Silas. 30 He then brought them out and asked, 'Sirs, what must I do to be saved?'"

Let us also reflect once again on the story of the Feeding of the Five Thousand, as we have already quoted and considered it in chapter 11, but from a praise perspective. The disciples looked at this small but very sacrificial gift and dismissed it as being insufficient, but Jesus thanked God for what they had and when the disciples distributed it to the vast crowd, it was more than enough. This story teaches us that when we face insufficiency of any kind – it could be finances, possessions or even physical health and emotional energy – instead of moaning and complaining about our insufficiency, we should thank God for the little that we do have and even give some away to others. The way in which we can apply this lesson to finances is obvious. However, we can also apply it to physical health and energy: instead of focusing on our pain or lack of energy, we should thank God for all the abilities that we do have and seek to do some act of kindness – however small – for others instead of looking to others to care for us. Scripture assures us that when we do so, our insufficiency will be more than enough for our needs. God's help and provision may not happen immediately, but if we persevere in faith, I believe that God will honour and respond positively to our demonstration of faith.

I would like to share a sermon illustration which gives a helpful insight into James' seemingly irrational teaching to consider it all joy when we pass through trials. The speaker was speaking in the UK but had been brought up in South Africa. He explained that they have oak trees in South Africa, just as we do in the UK. However, in direct contrast to the very valuable hardwood produced by oak trees in the UK, oak trees in South Africa only produce much less-valuable softwood. The reason for this is found in the rings of these two trees which show that the growth of the UK tree is reduced during the cold winters, thus producing a harder, more dense wood whereas the South Africa tree grows much faster in the continual heat and lacks the density of the UK tree. In a similar way, trials can produce strength and maturity in our lives.

Let us also consider why this choice to speak positively and gratefully even in difficult circumstances has such beneficial consequences. We have already learned that following their continual moaning and complaining every time that the Israelites faced a variety of different hardships, only two of them entered the Promised Land. So why did their moaning and complaining have just disastrous consequences? In James chapter 3, the writer teaches us about the power which is released following the words which we speak and warns us of the significant damage that can be done when we speak negatively. This teaching on the power of our words was not new, for it is also taught in the Old Testament. In fact, both Old and New Testaments tell us clearly that the words that we speak have the power both to bless and to curse.

James 3:5-10: "[5] Likewise, the tongue is a small part of the body, but it makes great boasts. Consider what a great forest is set on fire by a small spark. [6] The tongue also is a fire, a world of evil among the parts of the body. It corrupts the whole body, sets the whole course of one's life on fire, and is itself set on fire by hell. [7] All kinds of animals, birds, reptiles and sea creatures are being tamed and have been tamed by mankind, [8] but no human being can tame the tongue. It is a restless evil, full of deadly poison. [9] With the tongue we praise our Lord and Father, and with it we curse human beings, who have been made in God's likeness. [10] Out of the same mouth come praise and cursing. My brothers and sisters, this should not be."

In the Old Testament we find three themes showing the power of words. First: God created the world through the words that He spoke – and we have been created in His image. Second: there was the tradition of fathers speaking a word of blessing on their children. Third: God pronounced blessings for obedience and curses for disobedience. In the New Testament, Jesus tells us to bless and not curse those who hurt us.

In some cultures where spiritual belief is still dominant, this faith in the power of words is still just as real as it was in biblical times. In other cultures, with a more materialistic and worldly way of thinking, this concept may seem very strange. Whatever the belief in the region and culture where we live, the truth is that we all have tremendous power to do either good or evil with the words which we speak. Many of us speak without thinking about the consequences of what we say, and we are often oblivious to the harm that we are doing with our mouths, much of which is inflicted on ourselves.

When we face trials and testing and as a result focus on and speak about our pain, suffering and insufficiency, we speak words which effectively put a curse on our lives. We think that by speaking about our lack of finances or possessions or go into graphic detail about any health or emotional issues which we face, that we will gain sympathy and help from others. The very opposite is true for negative words have the power to strengthen and increase the difficulties which we face.

We have seen how praise and worship can release God's power in Malawi. At the beginning of 2017, the Lower Shire was attacked by the fall armyworm and communities lost 70 per cent of their crops. The African armyworm is a known pest in Africa, but it dies out naturally during the colder season. This fall armyworm, however, was thought to have come from America and could tolerate a colder climate. We visited Malawi later that year and suggested that church congregations go out into their fields to praise God, declaring out His sovereignty over this pest. We understand that where congregations did this in a committed and regular way, they had no further problems with this very destructive worm.

The following year, Lameck told me that many churches had continued to praise God in their fields even though there was no armyworm, and where they have done so, the rains have been exceptionally good, so much so that they have differed even from village to village and chiefs and communities from neighbouring villages have asked the church to come and pray in their fields. They have called this miracle "Faith in Action Fertiliser"! News about this demonstration of God's wonderful love, power and presence has spread widely throughout the region and should bring many more people into the kingdom as a result.

Chapter 24

Let God Carry You

Deuteronomy 1:30-33: "³⁰ 'The LORD your God, who is going before you, will fight for you, as he did for you in Egypt, before your very eyes, ³¹ and in the wilderness. There you saw how the LORD your God carried you, as a father carries his son, all the way you went until you reached this place.' ³² In spite of this, you did not trust in the LORD your God, ³³ who went ahead of you on your journey, in fire by night and in a cloud by day, to search out places for you to camp and to show you the way you should go."

Deuteronomy 33:27: "The eternal God is your refuge, and underneath are the everlasting arms. He will drive out your enemies before you, saying, 'Destroy them!'"

I used to be a member of the ladies' ministry team in my previous church. We were a group of six and we arranged a variety of events for ladies, both church members and non-church members. One day we were meeting together in order to prepare for a forthcoming event. Just before the break for lunch, the leader of this group suggested that we stand in a circle and pray, in turn, for the lady on our right.

As we were praying, I saw God cradling the lady to my right in His arms, just as a mother would hold a baby. I felt that He was saying that she was about to go through a difficult and testing time but that He would carry her through it. I saw weeds and thistles on the ground, but she was being held above them so that they did not hurt her. Upon sharing this picture and my understanding of what it meant, this lady started to cry. She shared with us all that she had woken up during the previous night feeling a pain in her breast, and upon looking in the bathroom mirror had found a lump. She went on to add that she had phoned the local surgery that morning and had made an appointment to see her doctor for the following day.

She later shared with me how my word to her that day had been just a part of the most wonderful demonstration of God's love and care. She is also a member of a prayer ministry team and prays regularly for people who contact this prayer line by telephone. Apparently, the week before we had prayed together, she had been praying for a lady and when she had finished praying, this lady shared almost the same picture as I had shared a week later. At that time, my friend did not understand its relevancy as she had not yet found the lump but when I gave the same picture a week later, this demonstration of God's love and care had moved her to tears.

However, this was not the end of this remarkable story. One week after we had all prayed together, she was talking to one of her twin sons on the telephone and was speaking to him about her present situation. However, although she had spoken to him about the medical aspects of recent events, she had not shared about these two similar pictures. She was amazed, therefore, when he told her that he had seen a picture of God cradling her in His arms. How can we ever doubt God's wonderful love and desire to care for each one of us?

You will not be surprised to read that her medical care proceeded smoothly and speedily without any problems or delays. Apparently, she had found the lump in its very early stage and the doctor was surprised and congratulated her for noticing it so early. However, one important aspect of this story was that she was able to walk through all her treatment without any anxiety or fear and with a peace and deep faith that God would undertake on her behalf, which He did because she believed Him to do so.

This event caused me to reflect on the scripture passages which speak about God carrying His people. Two of these are quoted at the beginning of this chapter. I started to ask myself why we so often deny ourselves this promised help and care and I realised that at the heart of this failure to do so, is a lack of trust in God.

When, for whatever reason, we find it difficult or impossible to put our trust totally in God's wonderful love for us, His good plans for us and His many promises to provide for us and to care for us, we will want to stay in control of our lives and to try to fix any problems which we face. Lacking deep faith in Him, we will put our trust in ourselves or other people. We may, of course, have been deeply hurt, abused and failed by other people and this makes trusting anyone else difficult. I believe that the greater the hardship and abuse that we have faced, the more we will try to stay in control of our lives to avoid any further potential hurt and pain. In direct contrast, those of us who have had the benefit of a loving and caring home will find it much easier to trust God.

If we allow anyone to carry us, we will no longer be able to control the direction which we take. This is one reason why we may not avail ourselves of God's care. If we are to walk closely with Him, we will need to follow Him wherever He goes. He will not follow us! Let us reflect on our earlier considerations about wading through the water flowing from the temple, as found in Ezekiel, chapter 47. When we walk through ankle-depth water, we are still in control of where we go but when we are out of our depth, we will be carried by the flow of the Holy Spirit. Similarly, if we allow God to carry us, we will no longer be able to control the direction which we take because our feet are no longer on the ground. It is this which we can find so difficult.

Following these considerations about God carrying us, I was speaking about this in Malawi with a view to encouraging everyone to trust in His wonderful love and care, and to allow Him to carry them, especially when times are difficult. Prior to this visit, my travelling companion had shared about our trip on social media and had received responses from about seventy people all over the world who said that they would pray for us. Immediately after speaking about God carrying us, my friend stood up to read a text message that she had received that very day from one of these prayer warriors. Although we had never met this lady and she knew nothing whatsoever about what I had planned to speak about, this text said that she was praying that God would carry us! There was, in fact, three occasions during that trip when we received a text message which confirmed what I had been speaking about.

There have been times when God has carried me in Malawi. It happens when circumstances are very hard and God just takes over, making a very difficult situation easy. When circumstances get harder and harder, you reach a point where suddenly everything gets easy even though the circumstances have not improved. If we reflect on this wonderful truth, it should be a wonderful antidote to fear and anxiety.

I will share four examples of this: the first was many years ago in Tanzania. I had been invited by the Mothers' Union, based in Dodoma, to be the speaker in one of their celebration events. It was very hot that day and there was to be a march through town immediately before the meeting at which I was due to speak. During this march, we were not able to stay in the shade and by the end of it I was extremely hot and very tired. Amazingly, when I stood up to speak, God just took over and thoughts and words flowed freely. Many people later commented on how good my word was. I can only say that it was good because it was God and not me.

The second two examples are very similar to each other: in both the weather was very hot. (The temperature can rise to over forty degrees centigrade in the Lower Shire.) In the first, I was attending a church meeting where we were sitting outside in the shade. Even though we were sitting in the shade, the temperature was so hot that I felt really dizzy and I found it difficult to stay upright with the scene before me spinning around. I was very concerned, realising that standing and speaking for about one hour would be far more difficult than sitting down. However, when I did stand, all the dizziness left instantly, and I had no further difficulty whatsoever. The second situation was similar: this time the meeting was held in a canvas tent and as soon as we entered it, I very nearly fell over because of the heat. Once again, as soon as I stood later to speak, all dizziness left immediately.

On the fourth occasion, the car had broken down about a mile from Nyamdheka Village where we were to hold a meeting. We agreed to leave the car and to walk the rest of the way. It was very hot and there were no clouds. I can remember speaking quietly to myself with every step: "I can do all things through Christ who strengthens me" and we arrived safely at our destination.

One way that we can build our faith and ability to trust in God's wonderful love and care is to speak positive biblical truth to ourselves on a regular basis. In direct contrast, we so often curse ourselves by doing exactly the opposite when we judge and criticise ourselves and focus on our weaknesses instead of our strengths. I wrote a poem about two years ago which speaks about God's amazing love and mercy. Reading this or any other similar biblical truth to ourselves on a regular basis will help us to allow Him to demonstrate that love to us.

This is how much God loves me:
His salvation transforms me,
His mercy forgives me,
His righteousness clothes me,
His love is poured into me,
His presence remains with me,
His arms are beneath me,
His peace guards me,
His rod and staff comfort me,
His victory delivers me,
His shadow covers and protects me,
His sanctification restores me,
His truth liberates me,
His spiritual gifts equip me,
His word sanctifies and guides me,
His grace enriches me,
His glory shines upon me,
His wisdom enlightens me,
His power strengthens me,
His blessing is spoken over me,
His Holy Spirit seals me,
His call envisions me,
His riches provide for me,
His goodness and mercy follow me,
His favour rests upon me,
His comfort sustains me,
His angels surround me
and His heavenly hosts fight for me.

Chapter 25

"I Was a Stranger"

Matthew 25:34-36: "[34] Then the King will say to those on his right, 'Come, you who are blessed by my Father; take your inheritance, the kingdom prepared for you since the creation of the world. [35] For I was hungry and you gave me something to eat, I was thirsty and you gave me something to drink, I was a stranger and you invited me in, [36] I needed clothes and you clothed me, I was ill and you looked after me, I was in prison and you came to visit me.'"

The fact that there are whole families living and working in rubbish dumps in Africa came to my attention through the ministry of two other present-day Christian organisations. Increasingly, I felt that this is a ministry which God wanted us to engage in. I shared this with Lameck prior to our trip to Malawi in 2018 and, with his encouragement, shared it with a group of about thirty area pastors, pastors and project co-ordinators. Almost immediately, this suggestion touched the heart of Wesley Msamange, Lameck's third son, and within a few days he had visited a dump on the outskirts of Blantyre and was profoundly moved by what he found there.

The first thing which hit him was the dreadful smell, mainly of rotting food. The second was the fact that there were mothers with babies on their backs and children playing in the rubbish which would almost certainly include the danger of used needles. The third was that people there were happily eating bread which was covered with mould.

He was not able to speak to the chairman of the group on his first visit because he was sick, probably from eating rotten food. However, he returned a few days later and was able to meet with him. They have since forged a wonderful relationship. When Wesley introduced himself, saying that he was from a local church, the chairman was amazed as no other church had done more than visit the site very briefly, never to return. To my mind, this is exactly where the church should be and certainly a place where Jesus would have gone. Surely, this is the very heart of the gospel, to go to places where others do not go, to people who are strangers and ostracised from society, to those who are considered poor, uneducated and insignificant, and to demonstrate God's love to them.

Following our return to the UK, we provided funds for eight weekly meals for all 350 inhabitants of this dump. We also provided funds for fifty bars of soap and later distributed some of the clothing which had been sent from England. Here is an edited version of two reports that Wesley sent us on this distribution of food, soap and clothing:

We were able to visit the rubbish dump and to provide these meals and through this kind gesture, we have been able to build a wonderful relationship and rapport with the people. They continue to be overwhelmed by such love shown to them and appreciate this act of love. One can see a sense of brightness and contentment in them. The impact of this ministry is so great, and it has brought hope to their lives.

The soap and clothing distribution also went well. This really will help to encourage this community in personal hygiene. During the distribution, they could not believe that this was happening. Everyone was just shouting, "zikomo – zikomo" ("thank you – thank you"). I also managed to speak to them about God's love. This really blessed them and at the end, many raised their hands so that we could pray with them. A few have said that they want to accept Jesus as their personal Saviour and want Him to deliver them from addiction of alcohol and marijuana.

One of the men stood in front of the whole group and testified that the message of God's love had restored hope and strength to him. He even said that he was considering suicide because of how tough things had been. But this message and demonstration of God's love has given him hope and has taken the suicide thoughts away. Wezi [Wesley's wife] and I also spent some time counselling him. Several of them have requested that we arrange for them to visit the Blantyre church.

Following this initial provision of food, soap and clothing, we started to prepare for setting up businesses, provided by a loan, which would enable this community to leave the dump for good. We have been providing small business loans for village congregations for several years. As this community is very close-knit – rather like a family – we thought that it would be more appropriate to set up businesses which were run by a group of five people. In this way, they will be able to continue their relationships with at least some of their friends.

We have been fortunate because Lameck's second son, Lawrence, has been running a successful business for many years and his wife, Enner, has been a member of a business-loan group and has gained much experience in setting up businesses and repaying loans. She, together with four other ladies from her group, have therefore been able to spend time teaching the rubbish dump community everything that they will need to know which will enable them to run these businesses successfully.

At the time of writing, this ministry has only been in operation for about two years and so I am not able to include a report of its long-term success. We have now, however, been able to provide funds for eleven businesses. Each of these businesses supports a group of five people from the rubbish dump. We started with three different kinds of business: first, restaurants at a total cost of £880 each and this includes funds for an initial rental payment as well as for stock and training. Second, groceries at a total cost of £811 each and this also includes a first rental payment, stock, and training. Third, electrical appliance shops at a total cost of £1,135 each and this includes training for servicing and mending electrical equipment as well as the first month's rental and stock. To date we have set up three restaurants and groceries and two electrical appliance shops. All these businesses have been set up successfully and are doing well. The members of each team have also been able to rent accommodation outside the dump, some sharing with each other.

Shortly after setting up our first two businesses, Wesley contacted me to tell me that another twenty-three people had recently come to live on the rubbish dump and one of them was a disabled lady who was restricted to a wheelchair. Wesley was especially concerned with her plight as he said that it was hard enough for an able-bodied person to scavenge for items to sell but for her, crawling on all fours and trying to find things of value or for food, was almost impossible. Wesley had spoken to her about what business she would consider viable and she said that she is a good cook and has always wanted to cook potato pieces and fry buns for students at the primary school near her home. This would bring her some income and she would not have to travel far. She is currently struggling with getting someone to push her around the rubbish dump as the paths there are not wheelchair friendly. We suggested that she worked together with an able-bodied person in this business and she has readily agreed to this suggestion. A short time later, we transferred just £271 for this business. This is not much to radically change two people's lives.

More recently, we have set up a fifth type of business which we have called a Trading Centre. After reading of the electrical appliance shop selling second-hand laptops for a commission, and realising that, although I can count thirteen charity shops in our relatively affluent town of Crawley, I have never seen a charity shop in Africa where the need is so much greater, I thought that there would be significant potential in setting up something similar in Malawi.

I made this suggestion to three church leaders in Malawi, and after they had discussed this with a larger team in Malawi, they replied that they thought that this would work well. I believe that the title "Trading Centre" is an accurate description of how this African version of a charity shop would work. People who need to raise some funds or who have items that they no longer need, will be able to bring them into this shop for them to be sold, and the shop will charge a commission of 20 per cent for doing so. The donor will only receive the money when the items are sold. The goods for sale will include clothing, bedding and smaller household and kitchen items (not larger pieces of furniture). There will also be a fitting room with a mirror where clothing can be tried on.

It will be necessary to keep detailed and accurate records: first, each item for sale will be given a reference number to differentiate between one dish and another. Second, a label will be attached to each item with the reference number and agreed sale price. Third, a book will be kept with each for-sale item listed with columns for the name of the donor, their contact details, agreed sale price and commission, a tick when the item is sold, another tick when the donor has been contacted, and a signature when money is received by the donor.

This centre will provide significant help for three groups of people: first the team who run the shop. Second, people who need to raise some funds and who have items that they no longer need. Third, families who need items but cannot afford to buy them new.

To date we have funded two trading centres in Malawi and one in Zimbabwe. The cost for setting up the first one was MK1,360,000 (£1,432). This included funds for advertising on the radio and in the newspapers as this was a new concept. We also provided funds for four months' rent instead of just one to give this shop time to become known. The second shop was cheaper and cost £1,000. It included the first months' rent, training and all the fixtures and fittings in the shop. Both these centres have been extremely successful.

We are aware that we have only visited one such municipal refuse site and that most major towns will have at least one, if not more. We are also aware that as we hopefully enable groups to leave each dump, that more people will probably start living and working there. Any such ministry is not, therefore, for the faint-hearted but – with God's help – we plan to see this as a long-term commitment. I can only add that knowing that we can change so many people's lives – both spiritually and physically – in such a significant way for relatively small amounts of money is extremely satisfying and rewarding. The greater the deprivation of those we minister to, the more dramatic the transformation achieved by such a ministry.

Chapter 26

Let Us Go Even Lower

Philippians 2:5-11: "⁵ In your relationships with one another, have the same mindset as Christ Jesus; ⁶ who, being in very nature God, did not consider equality with God something to be used to his own advantage; ⁷ rather, he made himself nothing by taking the very nature of a servant, being made in human likeness. ⁸ And being found in appearance as a man, he humbled himself by becoming obedient to death – even death on a cross! ⁹ Therefore God exalted him to the highest place and gave him the name that is above every name, ¹⁰ that at the name of Jesus every knee should bow, in heaven and on earth and under the earth, ¹¹ and every tongue acknowledge that Jesus Christ is Lord, to the glory of God the Father."

I want to look once again at the very important subject of humility. We considered in an earlier chapter how "the way up is down". In this chapter I want to consider this subject from a slightly different perspective, and this is how it relates to our relationship with God, other people and ourselves.

We so often think that if we were given a higher position of power and authority, then we could achieve so much more for God. Nothing could be further from biblical truth. We only need look at the life of Jesus to emphasise this challenging fact! Jesus achieved far more for humankind during His life than any man or woman in human history, and yet He was not born in a palace but in a humble and probably smelly stable. His parents were not wealthy but very poor. He held no official position within the synagogue. During His three years of ministry, He rarely had a comfortable place to lay His head at night. He took the place of a lowly and humble servant and washed His disciples' feet. He certainly did not have a large wardrobe of fine clothes although His one garment was of good quality. Added to all this, He faced the extremely painful and shameful death of a common criminal on a cross and was even buried in a borrowed tomb. How is it possible for us to look at His life and then aspire to a high position!

One way that we can measure Christian maturity is by our relationships and behaviour with both God and other people. Where is our focus? Is it on God, others or self? Satan can so easily deceive us in this area: he condemns us for our sinfulness and in this way draws our focus onto ourselves. We can be deceived because it appears humble to recognise our weakness and failures, and there are times when it is appropriate to do so, but if we are continually looking at our sinfulness, then our focus is on self and not on God and His wonderful mercy and grace. Let us therefore ask ourselves: what are our goals? Are we trying to lift ourselves? Or do we seek to honour and worship God and then to lift and encourage others?

Some time ago, God showed me a very simple picture: He showed me that if we want to lift an object safely, we need to place our hands beneath it. In direct contrast, if we try to lift something from above, we are very likely to drop it. This is true in our Christian life as well. If we truly want to lift and worship God, we need to humble ourselves and recognise our nothingness without Him. Equally, we will never succeed in lifting and encouraging others to fulfil their potential in God if we are still trying to promote and exalt ourselves. Once again, Jesus gives us the most perfect example: He rescued and lifted us by humbling Himself.

As we have already considered in an earlier chapter, one reason why our treatment of other people is so hugely important is because in different passages throughout the New Testament God promises to treat us in the same way as we treat others. Let us look at four examples. First, Jesus warns us that God will only forgive us for our sins if we also forgive others for their sin towards us. Second, He tells us not to judge others and warns us that God will judge us in the same way as we judge others. Third, Jesus exhorts us to be generous with our help and financial gifts towards others, promising that we will receive substantial financial support and help if we first help others and that we will receive help in the same measure that we give help. Fourth, Peter advises husbands to show honour and respect to their wives so that their prayers may not be hindered.

> Matthew 6:14-15: "[14] For if you forgive other people when they sin against you, your heavenly Father will also forgive you. [15] But if you do not forgive others their sins, your Father will not forgive your sins."

Matthew 7:1-2: "[1] Do not judge, or you too will be judged. [2] For in the same way as you judge others, you will be judged, and with the measure you use, it will be measured to you."

Luke 6:37-38: "[37] Do not judge, and you will not be judged. Do not condemn, and you will not be condemned. Forgive, and you will be forgiven. [38] Give, and it will be given to you. A good measure, pressed down, shaken together and running over, will be poured into your lap. For with the measure you use, it will be measured to you."

1 Peter 3:7: "Husbands, in the same way be considerate as you live with your wives, and treat them with respect as the weaker partner and as heirs with you of the gracious gift of life, so that nothing will hinder your prayers."

The Bible makes it very clear that if we want to improve the quality of our own life, we should first work to improve the lives of other people. When we focus our attention on helping others, God will focus His attention on helping us. There is a general principle here that we need to take very seriously: if we want God to help us, we first need to show love, respect, honour and care to others.

Matthew 7:12: "So in everything, do to others what you would have them do to you, for this sums up the Law and the Prophets."

There is a second reason why any attempt to lift and promote ourselves will have disastrous consequences: Jesus' words, as quoted in an earlier chapter, warn us of the dire consequences of acting in this way: if we try to exalt ourselves then God will humble us, but if we humble ourselves then God will exalt us. Jesus confirms this in His parable of the Wedding Feast: if we take a place of honour we may be humbled and moved to a lower place, whereas if we take a lower place our host may move us to a better place.

Luke 14:7-11: "[7] When he noticed how the guests picked the places of honour at the table, he told them this parable: [8] 'When someone invites you to a wedding feast, do not take the place of honour, for a person more distinguished than you may have been invited. [9] If so, the host who invited both of you will come and say to you,

"Give this person your seat." Then, humiliated, you will have to take the least important place. [10] But when you are invited, take the lowest place, so that when your host comes, he will say to you, "Friend, move up to a better place." Then you will be honoured in the presence of all the other guests. [11] For all those who exalt themselves will be humbled, and those who humble themselves will be exalted.'"

Although it may not at first appear so, verse 11 also challenges us about our treatment of other people. We could phrase this warning and promise in a slightly different way. If we humiliate others to elevate ourselves, then God will treat us in the same way as we have treated them: He will humble us. In direct contrast, if we humble ourselves before God in worship and encourage and show honour and respect to others, God has promised to exalt us.

We see this truth acted out in the life of Jesus, as described in Paul's letter to the Philippians quoted at the beginning of this chapter and our brief consideration of the humility of Jesus. He did not hold on to His exalted position with God but humbled Himself and became like a servant. As a result, God has exalted Him to the highest place and given Him a name above every name. Let us seriously reflect on the truth that if Jesus humbled Himself, how much more is it necessary for us to do so!

There is a further warning: when we lift ourselves, we must maintain this position through our own efforts but when God exalts us, He will maintain our position of spiritual authority and fruitfulness even when others try to humiliate and demote us. Let us also remind ourselves of Peter's words:

1 Peter 5:5-6: "[5] In the same way, you who are younger, submit yourselves to your elders. All of you, clothe yourselves with humility towards one another, because, 'God opposes the proud but shows favour to the humble.' [6] Humble yourselves, therefore, under God's mighty hand, that he may lift you up in due time."

So how do we get to a place where we are able to humble ourselves without losing our self-respect and allowing others to abuse us? In my understanding, one significant key to humility is to receive a revelation of how much God loves us. When this knowledge moves from our head to our heart, this – in my experience – changes everything. I had been a Christian for forty years before I really grasped hold of this wonderful truth, but it should not take this length of time. Sadly, many Christians live their entire lives without coming to this life-transforming knowledge.

This deep knowledge of God's love for us has two very profound effects on our lives: first, we no longer feel the need to promote ourselves because we have a revelation of our true value and worth in God's eyes. We are therefore enabled to humble ourselves because we no longer need to prove anything to anybody. We only feel the need to promote ourselves when we are insecure and doubt our own value. Second, because we have a deep revelation of our value, we will not allow others to treat us disrespectfully and will have the courage to speak out appropriately when others humiliate and abuse us.

Since the day when this wonderful truth became real for me, I have been filled with an inexpressible joy throughout each day, even when facing stressful and difficult circumstances and nothing has been able to take this joy away. My attitude towards God has changed completely: I am so filled with a sense of God's great love for me that my heart is also filled with a deep love for Him and I am motivated to seek every opportunity to tell other people how wonderful He is. This all comes quite naturally and is not contrived because I am increasingly aware that there are so many things to thank Him for.

1 John 4:19: "We love because he first loved us."

My attitude towards others has also changed: I have been able to focus my attention on encouraging and showing interest in them, while – at the same time – standing up for myself when they undermine and abuse me. I have become more sensitive to how others might be feeling and whether they need encouragement. My attitude towards myself has also changed: I feel good about myself, take more care of my appearance and am confident that God will make my life effective and fruitful without my needing to promote or focus on myself. Every day since has been even more wonderful and fulfilling than before.

In direct contrast, when we seek to undermine others because we feel the need to lift ourselves, we confirm and strengthen our own insecurities. The more we try to promote ourselves, the more we undermine our faith that God will promote us, and the more we try to earn love from God and others, the more we confirm and strengthen our low opinion of ourselves. It is a vicious circle in which we can quickly spiral in a downwards direction.

Let us affirm once again this truth which we have learned: the way up in God's Kingdom is first down! We should never try to lift and promote ourselves but allow God to do this in His way and in His time. When we allow Him to do this for us, we can also depend on Him to maintain any position and blessing which He gives us; we will not need to maintain it for ourselves. It is a sad truth that when God leads us into a place of fruitfulness and blessing, others will try to take this position from us, and so we need to know that when God opens a door, then no one will be able to shut it. However, if we try to lift ourselves, He has no obligation to protect our self-elevated position.

> Revelation 3:8: "I know your deeds. See, I have placed before you an open door that no one can shut. I know that you have little strength, yet you have kept my word and have not denied my name."

Chapter 27

Channels of His Grace

1 Corinthians 1:26-31 "²⁶ Brothers and sisters, think of what you
were when you were called. Not many of you were wise by human
standards; not many were influential; not many were of noble birth.
²⁷ But God chose the foolish things of the world to shame the wise;
God chose the weak things of the world to shame the strong.
²⁸ God chose the lowly things of this world and the despised
things – and the things that are not – to nullify the things that are,
²⁹ so that no one may boast before him. ³⁰ It is because of him that
you are in Christ Jesus, who has become for us wisdom from
God – that is, our righteousness, holiness and redemption.
³¹ Therefore, as it is written: 'Let the one who boasts boast in
the Lord.'"

As I have looked back over the last forty plus years in order to write this
book, I am left open-mouthed in amazement at all that God has done for me
and through me. I recognise, of course, that there are many others who have
been used far more greatly by God and have paid a significantly greater price
for obedience than I have done. But when I consider my many weaknesses
and failures, I find it hard to believe what God has been able to do despite my
many flaws. I am therefore assured that if God can work through me, He can
work through anyone. I have learned that our ability to be fruitful for Him
has absolutely nothing whatsoever to do with our ability and has everything
to do with His magnificent grace and faithfulness.

This wonderful truth is confirmed in the passage quoted at the beginning of
this chapter in which Paul confirms that God chooses the foolish and weak to
shame the wise and the strong and He chooses the lowly and the despised to
nullify those who are highly esteemed. Our lack of ability does not therefore
limit in any way what He can achieve through us. He chooses those who are
not confident in their own ability so that they will trust in Him and not in
themselves and give God the glory rather than trying to take it for themselves.

God, I believe, longs to demonstrate His love and mercy to a hurting world
and is looking for channels through whom He can pour His blessing and

grace. The only requirement for an effective channel is that it must be prepared to be hollowed out in order to become a conduit for His power, and the more each channel is hollowed out, the greater the flow of His power through it. It is not, therefore, a matter of devising brilliant plans or developing our gifts and skills. It is purely a matter of surrender, of recognising our nothingness without Him, of allowing God the freedom to humble us and to empty us of "self", of being prepared to take very risky steps of obedience and in trusting that He will enable us to do everything that He ask of us.

I once heard a sermon illustration of this truth. It was a very long time ago and I cannot therefore remember all the details of the story, but it went something like this: there was a farmer whose crops were wilting through lack of rain. Knowing that there was a river nearby, he carefully considered how he could find a way to transfer the water from this river to his crops. As he was considering this, he noticed that there was a bamboo plant growing beside his fields. It was a magnificent plant, growing tall and strong with an abundance of green leaves waving in the light breeze. It towered over his crops and looked beautiful as the spring sunshine shone on all its leaves.

This, he thought, could be the answer to his need to water his crops. He therefore approached the plant and cut down ten stems with his knife. He trimmed off all the magnificent leaves and split the stems carefully in half down their entire length. He then hollowed out the centre of the stems and laid these split and hollowed stems on the ground so that the water from the river could flow along them to his crops.

This, I believe, describes the process by which God prepares us to be channels of the love, grace and power. He does not choose us because of our appearance, education, wealth or gifting. Instead, He looks for those who will allow Him complete freedom to work in their lives and to transform them into vessels which He can use for His glory. The wonderful truth about being used as a channel for God's presence, love and power, is that an effective channel gets very wet!

2 Corinthians 4:7-12: "[7] But we have this treasure in jars of clay to show that this all-surpassing power is from God and not from us.
[8] We are hard pressed on every side, but not crushed; perplexed,

but not in despair; [9] persecuted, but not abandoned; struck down, but not destroyed. [10] We always carry around in our body the death of Jesus, so that the life of Jesus may also be revealed in our body. [11] For we who are alive are always being given over to death for Jesus' sake, so that his life may also be revealed in our mortal body. [12] So then, death is at work in us, but life is at work in you."

If we are to be used as a channel of God's love and power, we do not only need to allow Him complete freedom to prepare us for this wonderfully exciting role, but we also need to be continually filled to overflowing with His loving presence. The truth is that we cannot give out His love until we have received it. As I quoted in the previous chapter: we love because He first loved us.

1 John 4:19: "We love because he first loved us."

I also wrote in the previous chapter of how a deep knowledge that we are loved by God changes everything, and how when we experience this love it becomes very natural to speak about how wonderful He is to others. We find one example of a person who had experienced God's love and had been radically changed by it in the Apostle Paul.

Philippians 3:7-8, 10-11: "[7] But whatever were gains to me I now consider loss for the sake of Christ. [8] What is more, I consider everything a loss because of the surpassing worth of knowing Christ Jesus my Lord, for whose sake I have lost all things. I consider them garbage, that I may gain Christ . . . [10] I want to know Christ – yes, to know the power of his resurrection and participation in his sufferings, becoming like him in his death, [11] and so, somehow, attaining to the resurrection from the dead."

We also find it in the Apostle John's description of himself in the gospel which he wrote:

John 13:23: "One of them, the disciple whom Jesus loved, was reclining next to him."

John 20:2: "So she came running to Simon Peter and the other disciple, the one Jesus loved, and said, 'They have taken the Lord out of the tomb, and we don't know where they have put him!'"

John 21:7: "Then the disciple whom Jesus loved said to Peter, 'It is the Lord!' As soon as Simon Peter heard him say, 'It is the Lord,' he wrapped his outer garment round him (for he had taken it off) and jumped into the water."

John 21:20: "Peter turned and saw that the disciple whom Jesus loved was following them. (This was the one who had leaned back against Jesus at the supper and had said, 'Lord, who is going to betray you?')"

I recently heard a sermon illustration which described God's love in a very effective way. The speaker was describing how he had travelled to France with a group of friends from his time at university and how one of these friends worked for a well-known brand of chocolate. She had therefore taken with her a very large quantity of chocolates for everyone in the group to enjoy throughout their stay. He went on to describe how there were so many chocolates of every kind and filling, that everyone in the group could eat as many as they liked and of the variety which they preferred without any worry that their own favourite would run out.

He contrasted it with how he and his wife would occasionally buy some chocolate for the family to enjoy while watching television in the evening. However, in this situation, they only bought one bar so that the sections of chocolate had to be carefully counted and the total divided exactly into four equal parts.

He went on to say that we, as believers, often treat God's love in the same way as his family's small supply of chocolate. We compete or judge or criticise each other, trying to be better in order to gain God's love. Alternatively, we struggle and strive in order to earn His love. Whereas, in direct contrast, God's love is more like the abundant supply that this speaker had seen in France. His love is extravagant and totally unlimited. We can never exhaust His supply and we certainly do not need to earn it or to compete with others in order to receive it.

Tragically, when we fail to comprehend the inexhaustible supply of God's love, our competitive and performance-based behaviour leads us to focus almost exclusively on self and robs us of the ability to be a channel of His love to others. I believe that the principle which we considered in a previous chapter about "giving and receiving" – that the measure which we give to others determines the measure that we ourselves receive – also applies to love. The more, therefore, that we demonstrate love to others, the more God will pour His love into our hearts and lives.

In conclusion, I hope that this testimony will demonstrate these wonderful truths: first, that God's love is inexhaustible. Second, that He is amazingly gracious; loving us and accepting us just as we are with all our faults and flaws. Third, that He chooses the foolish, the weak, the lowly and the despised to be channels of His love and power to a hurting and very needy world.

Further Resources by Sally Jeffree

The Power of Praise

100 Daily Devotions to Help Us to Live a Victorious Life of Praise

When life is difficult, it is even more important than ever to focus on what is good, positive, and worthy of praise. This will help us to believe that there is light at the end of the tunnel, to trust in God to turn our situation around, and to protect us from anxiety and depression. However, when life is hard, it can be difficult to find things to be thankful for.

These inspirational devotions have been written to help us to stay positive when everything around us appears to be negative. Day by day they will focus on the wonderful truths of our position in Christ, together with the blessings and benefits which Jesus has gained for us through His death on the cross. God's mercy and grace is so great that it is hard for us to fully comprehend how He has transformed our lives, lifting us to a place of spiritual authority and giving us the inner strength to persevere in tough times.

For more details, please contact:

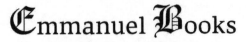

Emmanuel Books

Telephone: 01293 886596
Email: emmanuelbooks2020@gmail.com